Niger

Niger

BY BARBARA A. SOMERVILL

Enchantment of the World™
Second Series

CHILDREN'S PRESS®

An Imprint of Scholastic Inc.

Frontispiece: **Camel caravan in the Ténéré Desert**

Consultant: Adeline Masquelier, PhD, Professor, Department of Anthropology, Tulane University, New Orleans, Louisiana

Please note: All statistics are as up-to-date as possible at the time of publication.

Book production by The Design Lab

Library of Congress Cataloging-in-Publication Data
Names: Somervill, Barbara A., author.
Title: Niger / by Barbara A. Somervill.
Description: New York : Children's Press, a division of Scholastic [2016] |
    Series: Enchantment of the world | Includes bibliographical references and index.
Identifiers: LCCN 2015045602 | ISBN 9780531218839 (library binding)
Subjects: LCSH: Niger—Juvenile literature.
Classification: LCC DT547.22 .S66 2016 | DDC 966.26—dc23
LC record available at http://lccn.loc.gov/2015045602

1 2 3 4 5 6 7 8 9 10 R 26 25 24 23 22 21 20 19 18 17

Fulani woman

Contents

Left to right: **Aïr and Ténéré National Nature Reserve, Tuareg mother and child, Cure Salée festival, carrying water, Wodaabe man**

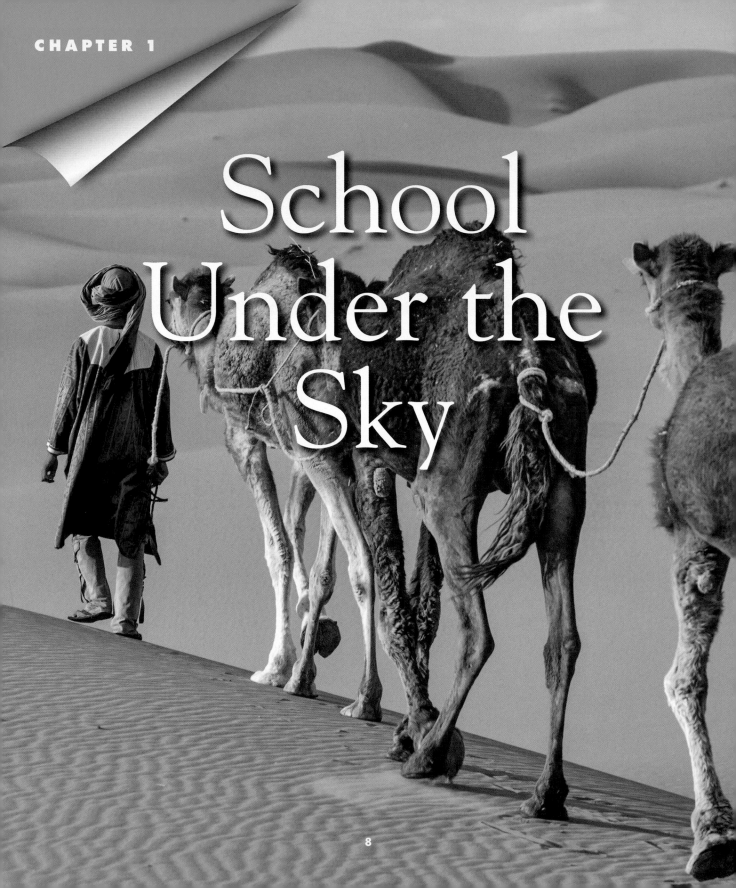

CHAPTER 1

School Under the Sky

TUAREG ARE TRADERS. THEIR ANCESTORS FOLLOWED five major trade routes across the Sahara, a vast desert that covers most of North Africa. Some Tuareg travel by camel, just as their forefathers did. Many others, however, now use four-wheel-drive trucks. In Niger, a country on the southern edge of the Sahara, the Tuareg cross the Ténéré Desert to Bilma. In Bilma, they collect salt, which they form into pillars. From Bilma, the Tuareg move south into the Sahel, the land near the Sahara that is a mix of grassland and wooded areas. There, they trade salt and dates for grain.

Boys and young men need to learn the business of their fathers. They need to know how to navigate across the desert from one oasis to the next. These are skills boys learn from their fathers in the open-air school.

Opposite: **The Tuareg live in desert and savanna regions of northern and western Africa. The largest numbers of Tuareg live in Niger and Mali.**

Nigeriens and Nigerians

The people of Niger are called Nigeriens. People from the neighboring country of Nigeria are called Nigerians.

A Tuareg group moves into the Aïr Mountains of Niger. The women set up tents and start cooking fires. The men tend camels, and the children go to school. This is not an ordinary school. A teacher sets up his classroom. There are no walls, and the ceiling is the blue sky. For a blackboard, the teacher uses a large rock.

Students sit in a circle and listen to the lessons. Most of the lesson this day is teaching children how to read Tamasheq, the

Many Tuareg people pack all their belongings onto donkeys or camels when they move camp.

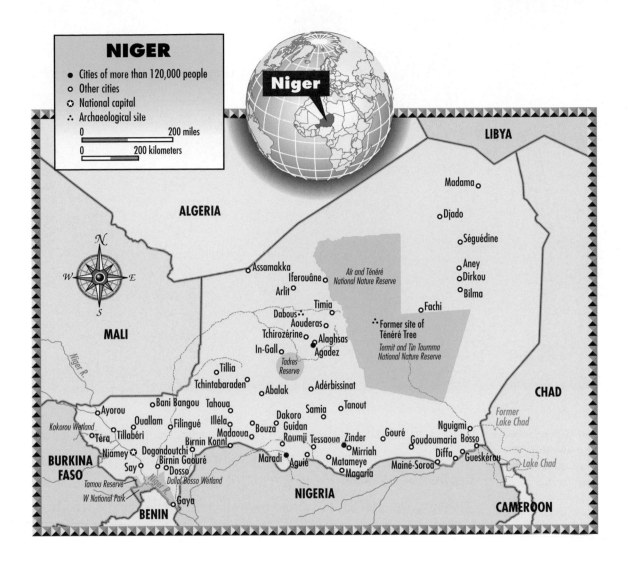

language of the Tuareg. The students practice reading short passages from the Qur'an, the holy book of Islam. The teacher also reviews basic mathematics. This will help boys and young men when they travel and trade their goods. Navigation, caring for livestock, collecting salt, and bargaining are subjects young men learn in their open-air school. They learn these skills by working with their fathers.

A group of Tuareg women cook in the evening. A grain called millet is their staple food.

Within the circle of tents, Tuareg women teach their daughters Tamasheq. The women own the family tent, the date palms on their land, and the livestock. They are responsible for passing on Tuareg customs, as well as their language, to their children. Girls attend a different open-air school from the boys. They, too, learn to read and write, but they also learn to cook, to collect and dry dates, and to maintain the family's holdings. They learn to make indigo dye from the bodies of sea urchins and to repair clothing pounded by the ever-shifting sands.

Sometimes, there is no time for schooling. The Tuareg begin moving at dawn and walk at least 30 miles (50 kilometers) a day across deep sand dunes and along the face of desert cliffs. At dusk, the people halt for a well-earned rest. While

Although Niger is in Africa, one of its national languages is French. A century ago, Niger was a colony of France. When Niger became an independent country, the government chose to keep French as its official language and the language used in dealing with foreign countries.

girls learn how to make millet porridge and strong, sweet tea, a young man sits at the feet of an experienced rope weaver. This, too, is a lesson. The people need rope for holding loads on camels and for tethering camels together. In the Tuareg open-air school, there are many lessons to be learned.

A Tuareg girl relaxes in her tent. An estimated nine hundred thousand Tuareg live in northern and western Africa.

CHAPTER 2

Sand and Sahel

IT IS NOVEMBER, AND THE TRADE WINDS BLOW COLD and dry across Niger. The wind is called the harmattan, and it comes every year. It blows throughout the dry season until March and carries grains of sand with each gust. The harmattan blows from the northeast or east, across all of western Africa. Day after day, the wind creates a dusty haze on the horizon. On occasion, the gusts develop into full-fledged sandstorms. When that happens, airplane flights are grounded, cars and trucks pull off the road, and even closed windows cannot keep the sand out of homes. The harmattan affects all Nigeriens. It is as much a part of the land as the mountains and the rivers.

Niger is a landlocked country of 489,678 square miles (1,267,000 sq km), about twice the size of France. The northern portion of the country is the Sahara Desert. The southern section is Sahel, a region with savannas (grasslands), wetlands, tropical forests, and dry zones.

Opposite: **A group of women make their way through a sandstorm in central Niger. Sandstorms can be dangerous, making it difficult to breathe.**

Erg of Bilma

An erg is a large, flat desert region of shifting windblown sand. The Erg of Bilma lies in the Ténéré Desert region of Niger's central Sahara. Located in the central-eastern area of Niger, the erg contains few towns. The largest is Fachi, an oasis with fewer than two thousand residents. The Erg of Bilma is a traditional home of Tuareg nomads.

Niger shares borders with seven countries. Algeria and Mali lie to the west, and Libya is directly north. Chad is to Niger's east. Nigeria lies beyond Niger's jagged southern border. To the southwest are Burkina Faso and Benin. Nearly all the borderlands between Niger and Algeria, Libya, and Chad are desert. The region bordering Nigeria, Benin, and Burkina Faso was originally grasslands and forest. Much of it has been cleared for agriculture.

Niger is a land of plateaus, desert plains, and sand dunes. The lowest point is found along the Niger River at 656 feet (200 meters). The highest point, Mount Idoûkâl-n-Taghès, rises to 6,634 feet (2,022 m) in the Aïr Mountains.

Sahara and Sahel

Today, the Sahara Desert covers four-fifths of Niger. Considered one of the harshest environments on the planet, the Sahara is extremely dry. Temperatures soar during the day but can be quite cold at night, after the sun has set. People have crossed the Sahara in camel caravans for centuries, moving from one oasis to the next. A growing number of travelers now rely on cars or trucks, though blowing sand can damage the engines.

Niger's Geographic Features

Area: 489,678 square miles (1,267,000 sq km)

Highest Elevation: Mount Idoûkâl -n-Taghès, 6,634 feet (2,022 m) above sea level

Lowest Elevation: Niger River (at the Nigerian border), 656 feet (200 m) above sea level

Largest Desert: Sahara

Longest River: Niger River, 342 miles (550 km) in Niger; total length of 2,600 miles (4,180 km)

Largest National Park: Termit & Tin Toumma National Nature Reserve, 37,500 square miles (97,000 sq km)

Average High Temperature: In Niamey, 106°F (41°C) in April; 91°F (33°C) in August

Average Low Temperature: In Niamey, 80°F (27°C) in April; 74°F (23°C) in August

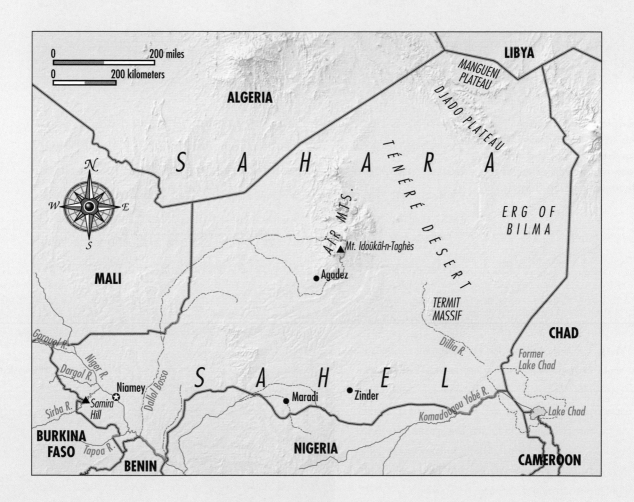

People wade through the streets of Agadez, in northern Niger. The rainy season sometimes causes devastating flooding.

Rain is rare in the Sahara, but when it does rain, it pours. Heavy rains flow off the land through dry riverbeds, called wadis. Sometimes, cloud cover fools thirsty travelers. Rain falls from the clouds, but the desert is so hot and dry that the drops evaporate before they touch the ground. This rain is called virga.

The Ténéré Desert is part of the Sahara and takes up much of the eastern-central region. The desert's name, which means

Art in the Desert

Where the desert meets the Aïr Mountains, at a site called Dabous, two large giraffes are carved into stone cliffs. These life-size carvings are considered some of the finest petroglyphs (carved stones) remaining from ancient times. Near the two giraffes are eight hundred smaller carvings of other animal species. It is believed that these petroglyphs were carved between eight thousand and ten thousand years ago.

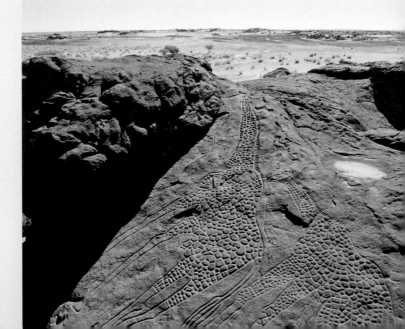

"where there is nothing," comes from the nomadic people that traveled Ténéré for more than two thousand years.

The Sahel is a zone that runs across northern Africa, directly below the Sahara. It is semiarid, hot, and usually capable of supporting farms and cattle. The Sahel is thought to be one of the poorest places on earth, a region in which the environment has been used and abused. In the Sahel, extreme weather can easily become a natural disaster. During a drought in the Sahel, plants wither and animals that depend on plants die. Famine can take over, and thousands of people go hungry. Heavy rains quickly turn into floods.

Fields of millet grow in the Sahel. The Sahel, which means "coast" in Arabic, got its name because it borders the Sahara like a coastline.

Animals find little to eat in the arid Ténéré Desert.

South of the Sahara, a zone of bushes and trees provides the Sahel with some protection from the growing desert. Desertification is slower in Niger than in other countries because of this plant growth. Unfortunately, people in this region often cut the trees for firewood. Goats, cattle, and wild animals graze on the shrubs. As the trees and shrubs disappear, there are fewer plant roots to hold the topsoil in place. The Sahara winds easily erode the unprotected topsoil, leaving nothing but dry, barren land.

The Aïr Mountains

The Aïr Mountains, which lie in the western Sahara, are sometimes called the Aïr Massif. A massif is a dense section of a mountain range that contains one or more peaks. The peaks in the Aïr range rise to elevations of more than 6,000 feet (1,800 m). The Aïr range has nine nearly circular massifs, which are bordered by sand dunes and the Ténéré Desert on the east.

The mountains have a mild climate, and their wide valleys receive more rain than the surrounding regions. This creates an isolated region that supports farms, towns, and wildlife. This rainfall and the protection of the mountains allow small towns to prosper and support farms.

A desolate massif rises from the surrounding flat land in the Aïr Mountains.

The oasis of Timia lies in the Aïr Mountains. It has a seasonal waterfall, and in a place as dry as Niger, a waterfall is a remarkable sight. During the rainy season, water pours through a ravine and into a guelta, a stone drainage area where seasonal water collects. Some gueltas in the Aïr Mountains have water all year long if a local spring feeds the pool. This local water source allows nearby farmers to grow fruit trees.

Lettuce and date palms grow in the lush Timia oasis in the Aïr Mountains.

Rivers and Lakes

Apart from a few seasonal rivers, Niger's main river network is made up of the Niger River and one smaller river, the Komadougou Yobé. The Niger River crosses the country in the southwest, covering 342 miles (550 km). But the Niger is the third-longest river in Africa, flowing 2,600 miles (4,180 km) through Guinea, Mali, Niger, Benin, and Nigeria. Midsized ships can travel a section of the river for part of the year and smaller canoes can travel it in the dry season. Nigeriens fish the river for perch and tiger fish. The river, like all of Niger, suffers during droughts. In 1985 and 1990, droughts caused shallow areas of the Niger to dry up completely.

The Komadougou Yobé River marks part of the boundary between Niger and Nigeria. The Komadougou Yobé begins in Nigeria and empties into Lake Chad, which lies where Niger, Nigeria, Chad, and Cameroon meet. Dams in Nigeria reduce the flow of water in the Komadougou Yobé and cause problems for farmers. They need the water for irrigation, but damming has reduced the water supply too much.

Boats in Niamey, Niger's capital. The Niger River divides the city in two.

Niger has a large number of dry riverbeds. In some places, these are called wadis. In the Hausa language spoken in parts of Niger, a dry riverbed is called a *dallol*. When the rainy season comes, water pours out of the desert and down the riverbeds in flash floods. It may seem odd that a place desperate for water suffers from flooding, but that is the case in much of Niger. The Dallol Bosso is a seasonal river that runs west and south from the Sahara to the Niger. Although this river truly flows only during the rainy season, there is underground water that can be accessed by drilling wells. Towns and villages have sprung up

Women draw water from a well in the Ténéré Desert. Wells are rare in the Ténéré, often hundreds of miles apart.

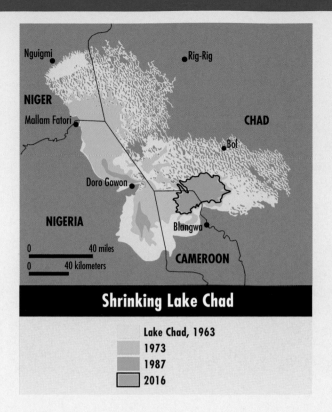

Shrinking Lake Chad

Lake Chad, 1963
- 1973
- 1987
- 2016

The Shrinking Lake

Lake Chad is a broad, shallow lake that once spanned the area where Niger, Nigeria, Chad, and Cameroon meet. But between 1963 and 1998, Lake Chad shrank by nearly 95 percent of its earlier area. More than sixty-eight million people depend on the lake for water, and although drought has caused the lake to shrink, scientists believe that half of the water loss is due to human water use. For example, people around the lake have drained water for crop irrigation.

Because of increased rainfall, the lake has grown since 1998, but water levels are still low and there is not enough water for the millions of people who need it. Although people in Niger still have access to the lake, the water levels are so low that there is no longer water in Niger's section of the lake basin.

along the Dallol Bosso because of the underground water. Flash flooding has sometimes washed away those same villages. Too much—or too little—water is always a problem in Niger.

Climate

Niger has one of the hottest climates in the world. In addition, there are three weather seasons: a very hot spring, a hot and wet summer, and a cold season that is not particularly cold.

In the Sahel region, rainfall is adequate and plant life thrives. Annual rainfall ranges from 4 to 8 inches (10 to 20 centimeters) in the northern Sahel to around 21 inches (54 cm) in Niamey. Niamey's climate is typical of the southern region. Daytime temperatures are usually high, frequently

Nigeriens run for shelter during a downpour in the Sahel. Parts of the northern Sahel receive as little as 4 inches (10 cm) of rain, while southern regions, such as Niamey, receive 20 inches (51 cm) or more.

topping 100 degrees Fahrenheit (38 degrees Celsius) from February to June. The most rain falls in July and August.

In the Sahara, rainfall never exceeds 5 inches (13 cm) a year. The city of Bilma in the Sahara has the distinction of having both the highest and lowest recorded temperatures in Niger. The highest was recorded on June 23, 2010, at 119°F (48°C). The lowest was 27°F (–3°C). There may have been hotter temperatures in the Sahara, but Bilma is the most northerly city where weather data is recorded. In Bilma, almost all of the rain falls in July, August, and September.

The southwestern corner of Niger is the wettest part of the country. In the city of Gaya, August is the rainiest month with rainfall averaging 9 inches (23 cm). Gaya does have rainfall in September and October, but November through February are bone dry.

Looking at Niger's Cities

Niamey, the capital of Niger, is also its largest city with a population of 774,235. Zinder, home to 191,424 people, is Niger's second-largest city. It is known for its dramatic architecture and sultan's palace. One of the ancient capitals of the Hausa people, Zinder features clay houses painted with beautiful decorations (right). At the city's daily market, Hausa farmers sell zebu, goats, and sheep. The city also has a regional museum that features such unique exhibits as large turtles and startling masks.

Maradi, with a population of 163,487, is Niger's third-largest city. Maradi was once built in a flood plain, but after being washed away several times, it was moved to a safer, drier plateau. The city is home to Hausa, Fulani, and Tuareg people, as well as a sizable group of immigrants from Nigeria. The city has a traditional handcrafts center, a central market, and a beautiful mosque. Maradi is also the heart of groundnut farming in Niger.

Niger's fourth-largest city, Agadez (below), is home to 124,324 people. Long a center for caravans traveling through the Sahara, Agadez features a mosque with an 89-foot-high (27 m) minaret made of dried mud brick. The city is a mix of ancient and modern buildings. Some are mud huts while others are elegant palaces. Agadez has long been a center of Tuareg culture.

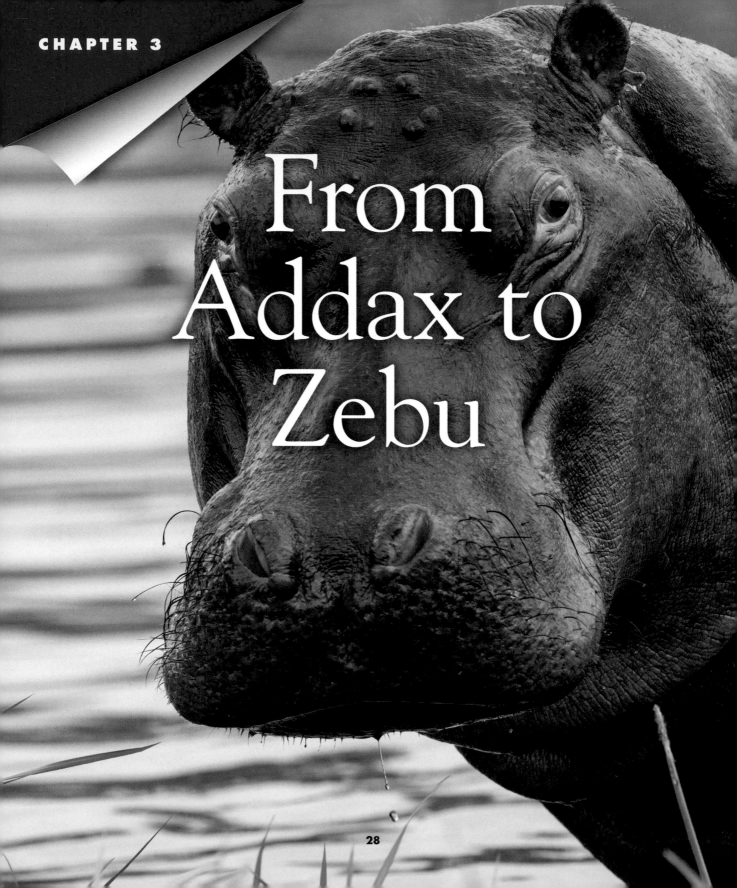

CHAPTER 3

From Addax to Zebu

IN A WADI IN THE TERMIT MASSIF REGION OF SOUTHEASTERN Niger, a cluster of addaxes munches on scrub brush and acacia leaves. The addax is the most endangered member of the antelope family. There are only four places left where addaxes live in the wild, and two of them are in Niger.

In southwestern Niger, a female cheetah eyes a single roan antelope entering the brush. She sinks low to the ground so that the antelope does not notice her. She has two hungry cubs to feed, and a roan antelope is a welcome feast. She creeps forward and attacks, but the antelope is too large for her to bring down. If her cubs are to feed today, she will have to settle for smaller prey.

In a grove on the outskirts of Niamey, hundreds of flying foxes hang upside down during the day. Flying foxes are fruit bats that feed on flowers, nectar, and fruit. When night falls, the bats take flight and look for a feast. African fruit bats are among the largest of Africa's bats.

Opposite: **Hippopotamuses spend about sixteen hours a day in the water, cooling themselves during the heat of the day. In Niger, some hippos relax in the Niger River.**

A National Treasure: Zebu

The zebu is also known as a humped cattle because it has a fatty hump on its shoulders, which is similar to the hump of a camel. Zebus are domesticated animals and are crucial to the survival of Nigeriens. They haul wagons like oxen do, provide meat and dairy products like cows do, and also provide hides, dung, and horns. The hides can be used to make all sorts of leather goods. Dried dung is excellent fuel for cooking and heating. Horns and bones are used to make knife handles.

Crocodiles have the strongest bite of any animal. They can easily grab and keep hold of antelopes, baboons, and other large creatures.

Niger's different regions provide environments for distinctly different populations of plants and animals. The Sahara hosts plants and animals that survive on little water. The wetter Sahel accommodates a variety of larger animals and plants.

In Wetlands and Savannas

Wildlife thrives in the wetlands, rivers, and farming regions of the Sahel. Many large creatures live near the Niger River, which cuts across the region. These include hippopotamuses, crocodiles, elephants, and giraffes. Hippopotamuses spend much of their time in the water. They may look sweet, but they are bad-tempered and dangerous. They sometimes overturn boats and kill humans and animals that they believe might be a danger to their calves. The Niger is also home to crocodiles that grow up to 20 feet (6 m) in length. They feed on antelopes and deer that come to the river to drink. Other daily visitors include elephants that eat up to 300 pounds (135 kilograms) of plant matter in a day. Rare peralta giraffes are found only in Niger, where they live side by side with farming communities. It is not unusual to see people harvesting millet in a field while a giraffe munches on the upper leaves of acacia trees nearby.

A Plague of Locusts

Although Nigerien farmers are often desperate for rain, it can have unfortunate effects. Sometimes, rain falls in desert wadis where locust larvae, the immature form of the insects, lie sleeping. The larvae need water to change into adults. When that change happens, the locusts swarm by the thousands. No crop, bush, or flower is safe as the hungry insects eat every bit of plant life they can find. In 2012, swarming locusts destroyed crops in Niger. Although the locusts are a feared pest that can threaten Nigeriens' food supply, they are also a source of protein. People collect them, fry them, and eat them as snacks.

The Sahel has both savannas and wetlands, which provide food, shelter, and nesting materials for a wide range of birds. Ferruginous ducks dip in river waters for small fish, while black-crowned cranes pluck their food from the shallows. Both Nubian and Stanley bustards and common grouse nest in the grasses of the Sahel's savannas. Five hundred and thirty species of birds make Niger their home at least part of the year. There are several types of raptors, including harriers, kestrels, owls, and snake eagles. Many species migrate to Niger each year from Europe during the rainy season. Temporary wetlands abound with insect life, which feeds many migrant bird species.

Black-crowned cranes are known for the stiff crown of straw-colored feathers atop their heads. The birds eat grasses, seeds, insects, and other small creatures.

The African baobab grows in dry regions of Africa. It can survive in the arid land because it has a wide-ranging root system and a broad trunk—sometimes more than 40 feet (12 m) across—that can store water.

In the southeast is a mix of savanna and forest. Kapok, shea, acacia, and baobab trees provide shade and housing for many animals living around the grasslands. The fruit of the shea tree is also an important source of nutrition for Nigeriens before the harvest, when food supplies are running short. Clumps of prickly grass and bunchgrass compete with long blades of elephant grass for space in the sun. In farmed areas, sorghum, maize (corn), and millet grow well amid the clusters of trees.

Squirrels, rabbits, rodents, and antelopes thrive in the grasslands. The presence of plant-eaters attracts predators. Lions are scarce, but there are cheetahs, striped hyenas, jackals, wild cats, and caracals. Caracals, a species of cat, are remarkably good hunters. They can jump high enough and quickly enough to catch birds taking flight.

Supersized Snakes

Niger is home to the African rock python, a constrictor-type snake that can grow more than 20 feet (6 m) long. Rock pythons are aggressive and attack any animal that it regards as food. This includes goats, gazelles, warthogs, crocodiles, and humans. Pythons live in grasslands, where they are close to water. In the long, hot summer, pythons take over another animal's burrow and estivate. Estivation is sleeping through a hot summer, much like hibernation is sleeping through a cold winter.

Life in the Desert

Dawn breaks over the Sahara. Small herds of addaxes browse on low-lying shrubs, wild olive trees, and Sahara myrtle in the Aïr Mountains. In the dune sea, a gecko stretches out on the sand to catch the sun's warmth. Farther north in Ténéré, a pair of golden jackals tears at the flesh of a dorcas gazelle that wandered too far from its herd. A rare Egyptian vulture circles overhead, waiting for its turn to feed.

In the Sahara, plant and animal life varies according to the landscape. The hilly regions are home to Barbary sheep, or aoudads, goatlike sheep that are sure-footed on the rockiest cliffs. Those same rocks provide nooks for rock hyraxes and perches for lesser kestrels, which feed on insects and small birds.

Niger's Aïr Mountains contain gueltas, pockets of water in rocky areas, that support both plants and animals the way other desert oases do. Olive and myrtle trees, Saharan cypress, and acacias grow beside gueltas. Antelopes, gazelles, and addaxes browse on the grasses growing nearby, attracting the attention of hungry predators. Striped hyenas and cheetahs prey on wild donkeys that come to the pools for water.

Sunset changes the Sahara. The temperature cools, and the desert comes to life. Fennec foxes leave their burrows in search of hedgehogs, eggs, and small lizards. Their huge ears allow them to hear the movement of both prey and predators. A deathstalker scorpion emerges from its nest in search of crickets or spiders. Tiny rodents called jerboas hop among shrubs, getting all the water they need from plants. The jerboas move quickly to avoid becoming dinner for any owls nearby.

A fennec fox stands by the entrance to its burrow in the Niger desert. The fennec's den, dug beneath the sand, is often long, with multiple entrances.

Species in Danger: Addax

Addaxes are large, tan-colored antelopes that are noted for their long, curved horns. They live in the Sahara but have become endangered because of hunting and drought. The addax's greatest enemy is humans. Since the development of jeeps, addaxes have been hunted for their meat, skin, and horns. Males weigh between 220 and 275 pounds (100 and 125 kg). Females are lighter, weighing 130 to 200 pounds (60 to 90 kg). Addaxes can live for a month without drinking water. They turn body fat to water and also get water from plants.

Replanting Forests

Across the Sahel, farmers commit part of their time and land to reforestation in a program started by the Nigerien government. This program, which began in the 1980s, has had a very positive effect in the region. As farmers plant their crops, they also plant some trees, which send roots deep into the ground and hold the soil in place. This program has resulted in trees being planted on 12 million acres (5 million hectares).

The trees that are planted must be able to grow with little rainfall and be compatible with the crops grown nearby. The types of trees grown include acacia, mahogany, tamarind, and kapok. These types of trees do not compete with grain for water or soil nutrients. In fact, they support grain growth. Many farmers have enjoyed increased grain crops where they have also planted acacias. Millet and groundnuts, for example, grow very well alongside acacia trees.

The Giving Tree

Tamarind trees provide Nigeriens with a host of products. The wood is excellent for carpentry, but the living tree is even more valuable. Tamarinds produce fruit used as flavoring in many dishes. Local healers use the pods for medicine, and tamarind also makes a surprisingly good metal polish.

Another 200 million trees have been planted apart from the program. The tree-planting effort has been successful in reducing topsoil erosion. It has also slowed the expansion of the Sahara Desert into cropland.

Conservation and the Environment

The Nigerien government established a number of nature preserves and national parks to safeguard the country's unique mix of wildlife. About 16.7 percent of the country's land is committed to conservation. The largest reserve in Niger—and all of Africa—is the Termit & Tin Toumma National Nature Reserve. It covers 37,500 square miles (97,000 sq km) of rug-

Lonely Tree

For years, a single acacia tree stood on its own in the Ténéré desert, 250 miles (402 km) from any other tree. The Ténéré tree was so distinctive that it served as a landmark for traveling Tuareg. In fact, it was often included on maps of the area. The tree, a short 10 feet (3 m) high, survived due to its extremely long root system, stretching more than 100 feet (30 m) down to the water table. Scientists believed the tree to be nearly three hundred years old. In 1973, tragedy struck when a driver ran into the acacia tree with a truck, knocking it over. The tree's remains were put on display at the National Museum of Niger in Niger's capital.

The Aïr and Ténéré National Nature Reserve protects the Aïr Mountains and part of the surrounding Ténéré Desert. Endangered animals such as addaxes, Barbary sheep, and cheetahs live there.

ged desert land in eastern Niger. Other protected areas include the Aïr and Ténéré National Nature Reserve, Tamou Reserve, Tadres Reserve, Dallol Bosso Wetland, Kokorou Wetland, and W National Park.

In the Sahara, dama gazelles, slender-horned gazelles, dorcas gazelles, and addaxes are among the animals protected in the Aïr and Ténéré National Nature Reserve. To the west of the mountains, a small flock of ostriches, numbering around two hundred individuals, are the last remaining wild ostriches in Niger.

W National Park is a transition zone made up of both forest and grasslands. Olive baboons, white-faced whistling ducks, and kobus are among the more unusual species in W National Park. There are also a few lions, cheetahs, buffaloes, and elephants near the Tapoa River.

Although the government has established reserves to safeguard endangered and threatened species, poaching, or illegal hunting, still occurs. There are not enough park rangers, nor is there enough money, to truly protect wildlife from poaching. Further threats come from the competition between animals and humans for the limited supplies of water and food in the area. During times of severe drought, all animals and plants suffer, and starvation is always a threat.

Although Niger has been making an effort to regrow forests, people sometimes cut the newly planted trees because they are so desperate for firewood.

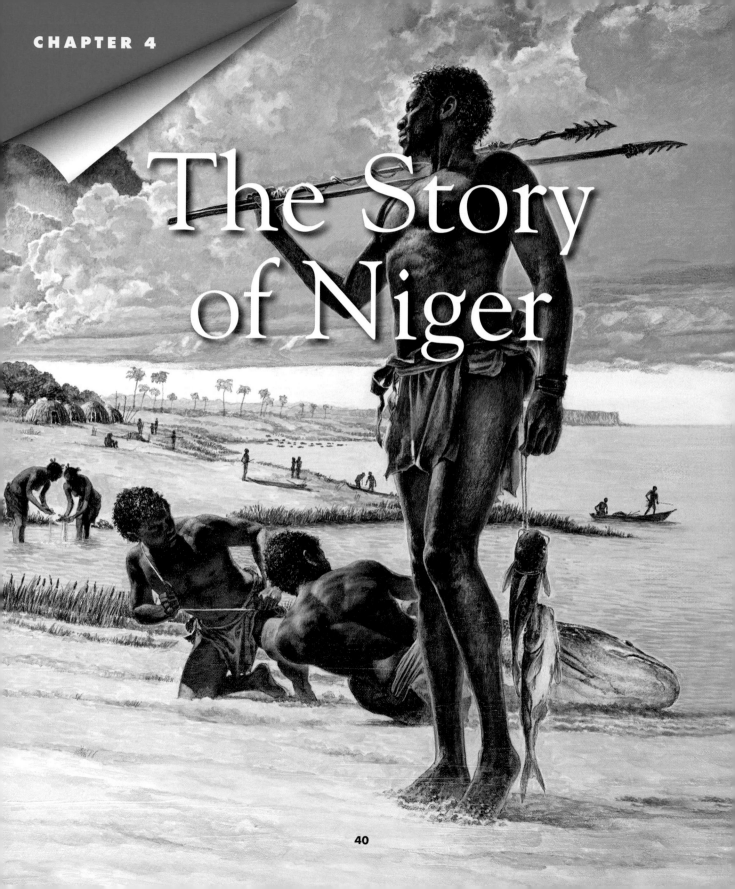

CHAPTER 4

The Story of Niger

ALTHOUGH TODAY NIGER IS 80 PERCENT DESERT, when humans first arrived in the area about ten thousand years ago the land was a tropical forest. Those first people were called Kiffians, and they were hunter-gatherers. At the time, there was plenty to hunt, fish, and gather. For about two thousand years, the Kiffians lived in what is now the Ténéré Desert. Then, in 6000 BCE, the region suffered a long-term drought, and the Kiffians moved away.

This severe drought lasted for more than a thousand years. When it finally subsided in about 5000 BCE, the Tenerians moved into the region. The Tenerians were also hunter-gatherers, although the animal species they hunted were different from the animals the Kiffians ate. The Tenerians had domesticated cattle. They fished in local lakes. They made jewelry from hippo tusks and fashioned cooking and storage pots from clay.

Opposite: **The Kiffians thrived in the land that became Niger. At the time, the region produced abundant food, and many Kiffians grew more than 6 feet (2 m) tall.**

Hausaland included seven principle states and seven outlying satellite states. The Hausa states were allies but independent, without an overarching political leadership.

By 4000 BCE, the climate changed again. Niger's lush forests gave way to the growing Sahara Desert. The Tenerians left, most likely following game they hunted for food. The desert continued to spread, and new people arrived in the region. For several thousand years, nomads who moved from place to place inhabited what is now Niger. And the desert expanded, and expanded.

More Migrations

During the tenth century CE, the Hausa people moved into present-day Niger. They were a collection of several different groups of people who joined together into one culture under a common language. The Hausas established city-states, each with its own ruler. Their combined homeland covered part of southern Niger and northern Nigeria. The city-states formed a loose-knit nation sometimes called Hausaland.

Meanwhile, the Tuareg migrated into the northern desert region. They were nomads who moved from one oasis to another. The Tuareg traveled across the dunes, with their homes packed on the backs of camels. They brought everything with them as they moved: their tents, rugs, pots, cattle, goats, and much more. In the desert, they began collecting salt and trading it for food and other goods.

Around 1300, some Tuareg gave up their nomadic ways and established a city in Agadez. The city became a permanent trading post for caravans crossing the Sahara. One route through Agadez linked the Hausa city-state of Kano, in what is now northern Nigeria, with the distant Mediterranean Sea.

Agadez grew quickly as a trading center. By 1500, it was home to perhaps thirty thousand people.

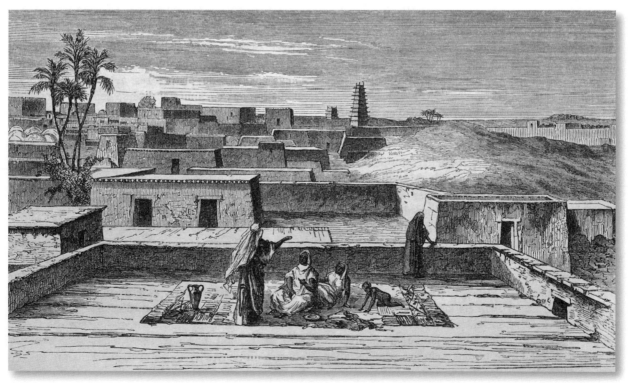

Powerful Empires

In the 1300s, the growing kingdom of Mali stretched its rule into what is now the western region of Niger. The people of the kingdom brought with them a belief in Islam, the religion that would mold Niger for centuries to come. In about 1375, the Songhai Empire rose to power. Within a century, the Songhai people expelled the Mali rulers and took over western Niger. The Songhai Empire dominated the region for more than two hundred years.

In southeastern Niger, the empire of Bornu (1380–1893) rose to power. It would become one of the longest lasting empires in West Africa. The Bornu became wealthy by participating in trade across the Sahara. In the late 1500s, Mai Idris

Bornu soldiers in ceremonial dress. The Bornu Empire was known for its horses, which were important in its military successes.

The Songhai Empire (1375–1591) was the greatest empire in West Africa before Europeans colonized Africa. The Songhai people introduced standard weights and measures. They established currency that could be used to purchase goods. They also selected qadis, or judges, to run a court system based on Islamic law, although the majority of Songhai citizens were not Muslims. Under ruler Sunni Ali Ber, Songhai became the first African kingdom to send government representatives to other Muslim states.

Alawma became ruler and Bornu became an aggressive military power. Bornu set up permanent military camps throughout the empire, which allowed it to protect itself from invaders. Idris Alawma introduced some innovative military concepts, including armored soldiers on horseback, troops on camels, and a navy on the Niger. Alawma established treaties with Egypt and the Ottoman Empire. Bornu grew rich by attacking enemy towns, selling captives as slaves, and trading cotton, kola nuts, ivory, wax, and animal hides.

In the early 1800s, Fulani forces began attacking the Hausa regions because they believed the Hausa kings were not practicing Islam properly. The Fulanis established an Islamic state called the Sokoto Caliphate in what are now

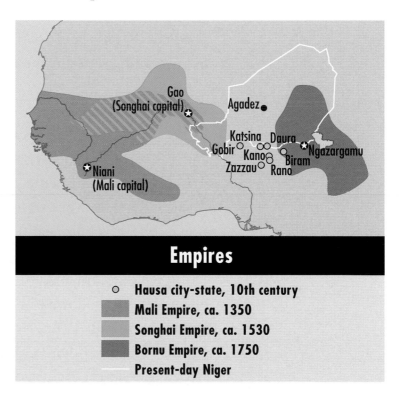

Empires

- ○ **Hausa city-state, 10th century**
- **Mali Empire, ca. 1350**
- **Songhai Empire, ca. 1530**
- **Bornu Empire, ca. 1750**
- **Present-day Niger**

Prior to their mission into Niger, Paul Voulet (front, second from left) and Julien Chanoine (front center) had been involved in other military expeditions in Africa. They already had a reputation for cruelty from their attack in 1896 on the Mossi people in what is now Burkina Faso.

northern Nigeria and southern Niger. It became one of the most powerful states in West Africa in the nineteenth century.

The French Arrive

In the 1600s, European countries reached south into Africa and began colonizing African nations under European rule. The French established a trading post at the mouth of the Senegal River, on the Atlantic Ocean, in 1638. True exploration of Niger by Europeans did not occur until the 1800s. The first explorer was Mungo Park, a Scottish adventurer who, in 1805 and 1806, traveled the Niger River through what is now Niger. He was followed by Heinrich Barth, a German, who wrote a book called *Travels and Discoveries in North and Central Africa*. European rulers became interested in taking control of Africa to reap the rich harvest of wood, minerals, and goods available. The European powers—the United Kingdom, Germany, Belgium, France, Portugal, and Italy—carved up Africa and created colonies that they exploited.

In 1898, French military officers Paul Voulet and Julien Chanoine set out on an expedition into Niger to gain control of French territories in West Africa. The Voulet-Chanoine mission was one of the most notoriously violent expeditions in African colonial history. On the way to Zinder, the troops burned villages, looted food and supplies, and massacred thousands of men, women, and children. When news of the atrocities reached France, other French officers were sent to arrest Voulet and Chanoine. Voulet and Chanoine killed the leader of this group in 1899, but then they themselves were killed a few days later.

In 1900, the French set up the Military Territory of Zinder, which became the center of French influence in Niger. France

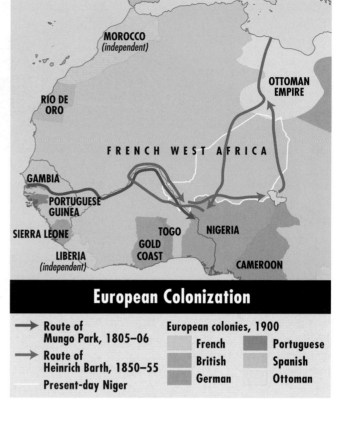

European Colonization

→ Route of Mungo Park, 1805–06
→ Route of Heinrich Barth, 1850–55
— Present-day Niger

European colonies, 1900
French
British
German
Portuguese
Spanish
Ottoman

The Warrior Queen

The Azna people, a Hausa group in what is now southwestern Niger, had a long tradition of female leaders. These leaders held the title *sarraounia*, which means "queen" or "female chief." The most famous Azna queen was Sarraounia Mangou. At the end of the 1800s, while Voulet and Chanoine terrorized villages on their march to Zinder, Mangou fought back. She and her Azna forces battled the French to protect her capital at Lougou. In 1986, Mangou was the subject of an award-winning film called *Sarraounia*.

In Niger in the early 1900s, mail was delivered by a person on camelback.

treated the people of Niger as if they were ignorant children. They set up schools in which students learned French reading and writing. Nigeriens were expected to wear French styles of clothing, although those clothes were not appropriate for the climate. Anyone who followed French ways was rewarded. Those who kept to their traditional cultures were mistreated. One example of this was the *corvée*, hard labor the French required every local male to perform. Corvée was like a tax, but instead of paying with money, citizens paid with work. The program was not much different from slavery, in that workers had no choice about working and were not paid. The work included constructing roads, rail lines, and government buildings.

Many Nigerien people fought against French rule. The Tuareg entered into several periods of rebellion. In 1916, they led a rebellion in the Aïr Mountain region and placed Agadez under siege. But efforts to oust the French were fruitless. The Tuareg had swords; the French had rifles and machine guns. The French declared Niger an official colony in 1922.

From 1946 to 1960, groups in Niger began pushing for independence. Gradually, the French responded. In 1946, Niger was allowed to elect a single representative to the French National Assembly. A group of privileged Nigeriens, called the *évolués* (meaning "evolved"), formed Niger's first political party, the Parti Progressiste Nigérien (PPN), founded by Hamani Diori. Diori worked with the other members of French West Africa who were also interested in gaining independence from France. In 1958, Niger's citizens voted for self-government while remaining part of the French Community in West Africa.

Hamani Diori was a member of the French National Assembly when Nigeriens voted for self-government in 1958. He then became the president of Niger's Council of Ministers, making him the head of the government.

Independence and Strife

Niger became independent in 1960, and Hamani Diori became president. Though it seemed that all Nigeriens were at last united, there were, in fact, many factors dividing the people. One factor was ethnic loyalty. The people still considered themselves Hausa, Tuareg, Zarma, Fulani, or members of other groups. In many cases, members of one ethnic group did not like having someone from another ethnic group as head of the government. In addition, many Nigeriens resented the évolués, who had sided with the French in language, education, dress, and habits. Nigeriens who had been imposed corvée labor felt that the évolués had turned their backs on their native culture and profited off the work of the oppressed. Finally, the politicians and the military often disagreed. The politicians had political power, but the military had weapons.

At first, Diori maintained close ties with the French. France provided support in terms of weapons, technology, and money. Still in its infancy, Niger needed France's help. Diori put his friends and faithful followers in positions of power. He managed the country with a combination of fatherly advice and crafty statesmanship. Diori would have stayed in office longer than fourteen years if it had not been for a prolonged drought.

During periods of famine, people sometimes rise up against a government that is not helping them. The army, following the lead of Lieutenant Colonel Seyni Kountché, overthrew Diori's presidency in what is called a military coup. Diori was imprisoned, and Kountché asked French troops to leave Niger.

By 1980, Niger was again looking forward to a democratic government. Ordinary citizens were allowed to join the Supreme Military Council administration. Another council was formed to advise the government about civil problems. This council worked much like the old National Assembly from Diori's presidency. Politician Mamane Oumarou was named prime minister and advisor to Chairman Kountché.

In 1983, another coup took place. During this coup, one military leader, Lieutenant Idrissa Amadou, waited until Chairman Seyni Kountché was in France to try to overthrow the government. This time, the coup failed. It was later revealed that Oumarou had arranged for the coup, and he was replaced as prime minister by Ahmid Algabid.

In 1987, Kountché died and was replaced by Colonel Ali Saibou, who began a transition to full democracy. Over the next few years, political parties rose up to represent varied interests in Niger. An election returned military leaders to power, and Saibou's National Movement for a Developing Society (MNSD) took all the seats in the National Assembly.

The Red Cross distributes food to children in Niger during a famine in the early 1970s.

Recent Times

The next decade was a mix of attempted coups, Tuareg upris-ings, and economic disasters. Niger went through another serious drought, which led to famine. Mahamane Ousmane, a member of a young party called the Democratic and Social Convention–Rahama, was elected president in 1993 in the midst of a decaying economy, student riots, a Tuareg uprising, and political worries. In January 1996, the military once again stepped in and removed the elected government from office. The coup's leader, General Ibrahim Baré Maïnassara, fixed the elections later in the year and declared himself victor.

Members of the military who overthrew Mamadou Tandja in 2010 speak to supporters in Niamey.

Baré was assassinated in 1999 and Mamadou Tandja won the presidential election. He won again in 2004, and in 2009 tried to change the constitution, which banned presidents from seeking a third term. He was ousted in a coup in February 2010 and a military government was set up until democratic order could be reestablished. In 2011, Mahamadou Issoufou won the presidential election. When he took the oath of office, civilian rule returned to Niger.

In 2015, Niger faced a new problem—raids by Boko Haram on Nigerien villages. Boko Haram is a violent band of extremists that wants to institute Islamic rule and conservative social practices. Boko Haram is noted for mass killings, kidnappings, and recruiting child soldiers. Niger's government has its army posted to fight Boko Haram, but the border is long, and attempts to fend off the raids are not always successful.

Thousands of Nigeriens rallied in Niamey in 2015 to show their support for Niger's fight against Boko Haram.

CHAPTER 5

Running the Country

Leading the Republic of Niger has never been an easy task. The country's economy is struggling, and famine and malnutrition are widespread. Because of the country's persistent problems, the government has been unstable. The Nigerien military has a history of staging coups and ousting elected leaders.

Niger is a republic with a president as the head of state and a prime minister as head of the government. The prime minister is appointed by the president. Niger has three major political parties: the Nigerien Party for Democracy and Socialism, the National Movement for a Developing Society, and the Nigerien Democratic Movement for an African Federation. A handful of smaller parties also exist.

Opposite: **Members of Niger's National Assembly listen to a speaker. Only 6 of the 109 members of the legislature are women.**

Niger's Flag

The national flag of Niger features three horizontal stripes in orange, white, and green. The orange represents the grasslands, the white stands for the Niger River, and the green is the country's rain forests. The large orange circle in the center stands for the sun. The flag was officially adopted in November 1959.

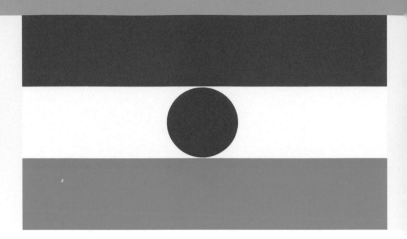

A woman votes in Niamey in 2016. All Nigeriens who are at least eighteen years old can vote.

The Constitution

Niger's constitution establishes an elected government and states the powers of each branch. Adopted in 2010, the constitution says that the government must support the rights of individuals, freedom, justice, equality, and safety.

Aminatou Gaoh (right) speaks to German chancellor Angela Merkel. Gaoh served as Niger's ambassador to Germany from 2012 to 2016.

Each Nigerien is entitled to the freedom to speak his or her language and follow a chosen religion. The constitution identifies voting rights as free, equal, secret, and universal. All Nigeriens who are eighteen years old are entitled to vote. Women and children are equal to men under law, and it is the duty of the government to support families and individuals equally.

Executive Branch

The head of state in the Republic of Niger is the president. To be elected president a person must be of Nigerien birth, at least thirty-five years old, and of good moral character. The president cannot be a leading member of any political party or hold any other job. He or she is elected for a five-year term and may run for two terms only. Election is by majority ballot in two rounds

Niger's president Mahamadou Issoufou was reelected in 2016.

of voting. If a candidate wins more than 50 percent of the vote in the first election, that candidate is declared president. If no one wins by a majority, a second vote is held with only the top two vote getters from the first election. President Mahamadou Issoufou was elected in 2011 in a two-part election.

The president has a number of responsibilities, including appointing the prime minister, who is the leader of the political party with the most seats in the National Assembly. The president is the Supreme Head of the Armies. It is also the president's duty to enforce the laws of Niger and to represent Niger's interests with other countries. The president signs ordinances, decrees, laws, and any state of emergency documents necessary for running the country.

A Council of Ministers advises the president on specific areas affecting the country. There are currently thirty-seven ministers, each with a specific area of responsibility. The minister of state deals with foreign affairs. The minister of agriculture is responsible for providing up-to-date information on farming and livestock.

Legislative Branch

The prime minister is considered the head of the government. He or she directs and coordinates government activities, such as budget planning, development, and lawmaking.

Nigerien army forces patrol in Niamey in 2016. The nation has about twelve thousand active-duty soldiers.

Representatives to the National Assembly are called deputies. Their term is for five years, but a special election is held when the president declares that the National Assembly is not working well. The assembly is dissolved and a new election for deputies is held.

Deputies must be Nigerien citizens and at least twenty-one years old. In total, there are 113 deputies, with 105 being elected from political parties and eight from minority groups. At least 10 percent of the members of the National Assembly must be women.

Brigi Rafini, Niger's prime minister, speaks at a conference in Europe. A member of the Nigerien Party for Democracy and Socialism, he became prime minister in 2011.

Deputies sit on committees that focus on a certain area. A deputy might sit on the Committee for National Defense or the Committee for Economics and Finance. The committees review proposed laws and write new bills to become laws. Deputies cannot pass any law that goes against rights provided by the constitution.

One of the rights held by the National Assembly is a declaration of war. The military or the president may recommend going to war, but only the National Assembly can say Niger is at war. Sending troops into battle must be voted on by the National Assembly. Other rights held by the National Assembly are developing a national budget and levying national taxes.

Supporters of President Mahamadou Issoufou cheer at a campaign rally in 2016. Many are wearing pink, the color of the Nigerien Party for Democracy and Socialism.

The Judicial Branch

Niger's judicial system is separate and independent from the legislative and the executive branches. Magistrates (judges) are independent and vow to uphold the law. Magistrates are appointed by the president of Niger, but they are suggested by the Minister of Justice.

Niger's National Anthem

The lyrics of "La Nigérienne" were written by Maurice Albert Thiriet and Robert Jacquet. Nicolas Abel François Frionnet wrote the music. The song was adopted as Niger's national anthem in 1961.

English translation

By the waters of the mighty Niger,
Which adds to the beauty of nature,
Let us be proud and grateful
For our new-won liberty.
Let us avoid vain quarreling,
So that our blood may be spared,
And may the glorious voice
Of our race, free from tutelage,
Rise unitedly, surging as from one man,
To the dazzling skies above,
Where its eternal soul, watching over us,
Brings greatness to the country.

Arise, Niger, arise! May our fruitful work
Rejuvenate the heart of this old continent,
And may this song resound around the world,
Like the cry of a just and valiant people.

Arise, Niger, arise! On land and river,
To the rhythm of the swelling drum-beats' sound,
May we ever be united and may each one of us
Answer the call of this noble future that says to us,
"Forward!"

We find again in our children
All the virtues of our ancestors.
Such virtues are our inspiration
For fighting at every moment.
We confront ferocious and treacherous animals
Often scarcely armed,
Seeking to live in dignity,
Not slaying with a lust to kill.
In the steppe where all feel thirst,
In the burning desert,
Let us march tirelessly forward
As magnanimous and vigilant masters.

Niger's National Government

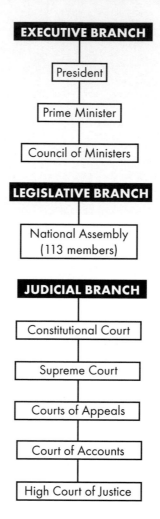

EXECUTIVE BRANCH

President

Prime Minister

Council of Ministers

LEGISLATIVE BRANCH

National Assembly
(113 members)

JUDICIAL BRANCH

Constitutional Court

Supreme Court

Courts of Appeals

Court of Accounts

High Court of Justice

The Constitutional Court has seven members, and all must be at least forty years old. The court has two people with professional experience as judges. Two more magistrates are chosen by other judges. One magistrate is a lawyer with ten years of experience. One magistrate is a law professor. The seventh magistrate represents one of the associations in Niger that promote legal or human rights. The magistrates on the Constitutional Court are appointed for a six-year term. The Constitutional Court rules on whether laws passed by the National Assembly follow Niger's constitution.

The Supreme Court is Niger's highest court regarding judicial matters. It hears appeals from lower courts. Niger also has eight Courts of Appeals, one in each of Niger's regions, which review lower court cases.

Other courts in Niger have responsibilities dealing with specific legal matters. The Court of Accounts deals with the spending of government money. The High Court of Justice handles cases in which public officials are accused of crimes.

Local Government

Most ethnic groups have their own internal government. They have a chief, whose position is inherited from his father or other male relatives. They may have a council of elders to

A Lawyer or Not?

There are two types of lawyers in Niger. An *avocat* (left) is a criminal or civil attorney. This person handles legal matters between clients and other parties. An avocat may represent a client accused of a crime when the case goes to trial.

For everyday matters, people see a *notaire*. This type of lawyer deals with wills, deeds, real estate problems, leases, mortgages, and business contracts. If a notaire's client has to go to court, an avocat is called on to represent the client. Notaires are not allowed to try court cases.

offer advice to the chief. A chief can act as a mediator or judge in cases that deal with community legal matters. Such matters would include marriages, inheritance issues, or land disputes. The chiefs are not official judges. They cannot try people for criminal matters, such as murder or robbery.

Customary courts are found in larger towns and small cities. The courts are limited to civil matters and follow Islamic law. Customary courts are led by a lawyer, a chief, or another person who knows local customs and traditions. Decisions made in customary courts can be appealed to a higher court.

A meeting of the town council in Timia

A Look at the Capital

Niamey, the capital of Niger, began as an agricultural village along the Niger River in the 1700s. It remained small until it became a French colonial outpost in the 1890s. In 1926, it became the capital of the Niger colony, and after that, it grew quickly. In recent years, many people have moved from rural areas into Niamey. Today, it is Niger's largest city, with a population of 774,235.

Niamey features large mosques and bustling markets. It is the site of many important institutions, including the University of Niamey and the National Museum of Niger, which introduces visitors to the varied cultures of Niger's ethnic groups and displays fossils of dinosaurs and other extinct creatures that once roamed the region.

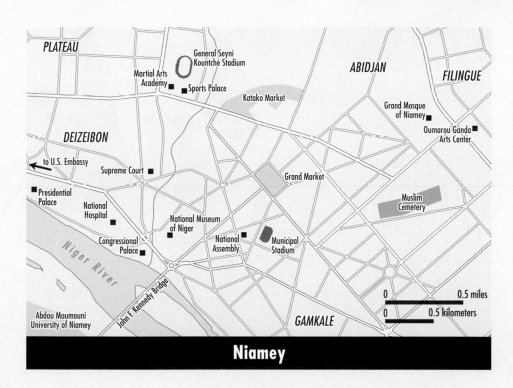

Niamey

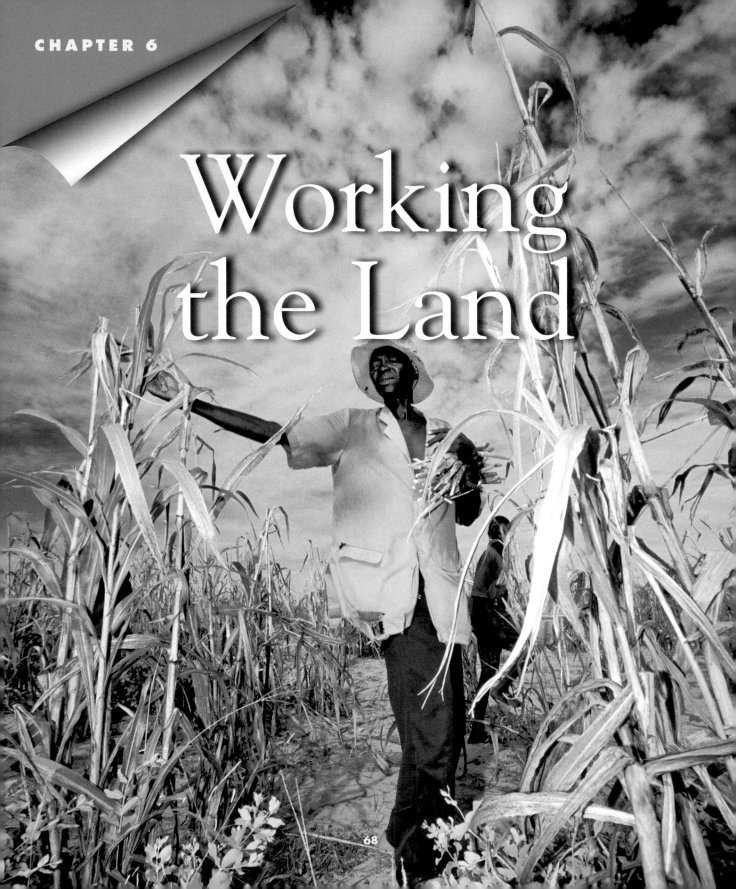

CHAPTER 6

Working the Land

ABDOU USES A FOOT PLOW TO CARVE THROUGH the dry topsoil of his farm. It is time to plant millet, and he hopes this year the rains will come. Abdou and his wife have five children: three boys and two girls. The youngest child is the only one who does not work on the farm. Traditionally, by the age of seven, Nigerien farm children work every day. There is not enough money for school, and the family needs the children to work. While Abdou plows, his sons dig holes for planting acacia trees. Abdou is one of many farmers taking part in the national reforestation program.

The millet Abdou grows will barely be enough to feed his family through the year. Millet makes up more than 65 percent of the food his family eats. Millet is a grain, much like wheat or oats. His wife and oldest daughter pound dried millet into flour to make bread. Whole grains are used to make porridge, served with goat milk. Millet mixed with water and sugarcane makes a nutritious drink that Nigeriens drink.

Opposite: **A farmer harvests millet. Millet is a tall grass with small seeds that are an important food source in Niger.**

The official currency of Niger is the West African franc, or CFA (Communauté Financière Africaine). The same currency is used by Mali, Burkina Faso, Guinea-Bissau, Senegal, Togo, Ivory Coast, and Benin. Currency and coins are produced in Senegal. Banknotes come in values of 1,000, 2,000, 5000, and 10,000 francs. Coins include 1, 5, 10, 25, 50, 100, 200, and 500 francs. All bills depict a carved wooden mask on the front, along with images of different segments of the economy. The reverse shows animals typical of West Africa. For example, the 2,000-franc note features transportation on the front and fish on the reverse, while the 5,000-franc note honors agriculture and antelopes. In 2016, 579.5 CFA francs equaled US$1.00.

Economic Struggles

Niger's economy depends heavily on agriculture. There is some mining and industry, but 95 percent of the labor force works in agriculture or raising livestock. Very little of Niger's land can be farmed. Most is desert or mountain areas. The major cities occupy some of the farmable land, which means less space for growing food.

In many ways, the health of Niger's economy depends on rainfall. In the past fifty years, prolonged droughts have reduced Niger's ability to grow crops. Today, Niger does not grow enough food to feed its people, and three out of five people live in poverty.

Niger is one of the lowest-income countries in the world. More than 2.5 million people in Niger regularly have too little

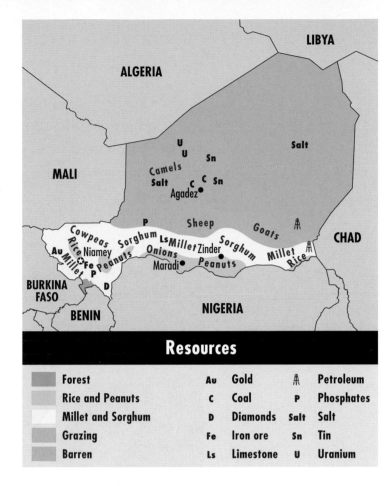

food available during good years. That number doubles in lean years. Four out of ten children are severely malnourished, which makes them more likely to die of either malnutrition or disease.

On most farms, people live with no electricity. They have no access to modern medicine or technology. In cities, workers do not fair much better. The average monthly salary of a person living in Niamey is 200,000 CFA francs, or about US$335. A one-bedroom apartment on the city's outskirts costs about 250,000 CFA francs per month. Water, electricity, heat, and garbage collection add another 142,500 CFA francs. Just having a place to live costs almost twice what a worker makes in the city. And those costs do not include food, clothing, or transportation.

Agriculture and Forestry

Agriculture in Niger is limited to the Sahel region, and even further limited to places where there is sufficient rainfall or groundwater. Eleven percent of the land is used to grow temporary crops, and 22 percent is pasture. Permanent crops are grown on 0.05 percent of the land.

The main crops produced in Niger are millet, cowpeas, and sorghum. Millet and sorghum are grains, while cowpeas are like black-eyed peas. Other crops grown in Niger include onions, peanuts, cabbages, tomatoes, and cassava. Fruits include mangoes, dates, and guavas. Some farmers plant fruit-bearing trees among their grain crops. Most farming is done on small individual farms, and most is subsistence farming. That is when a farming family lives on the crops it grows. Women work the fields and also plant kitchen gardens.

In the Sahel, Nigeriens grow vegetables that they sell at markets.

A boy herds goats back home at the end of the day. There are nearly fourteen million goats in Niger.

Keeping livestock is common, and owning livestock is a status symbol. Across the country, herders own 13,800,000 goats, 10,400,000 sheep, and 10,200,000 of a type of cattle called zebus. These animals provide milk, cheese, and, on occasion, meat. Most families cannot afford to slaughter their animals for meat, as they are more valuable for their milk. Zebus provide dairy and meat, but they are also used for plowing and hauling. Camels are extremely valuable as they are the most reliable means of transportation in the desert.

Forestry is a problem in Niger. Many people cook on wood fires, and 94 percent of families use harvested wood as their main source of fuel. The land desperately needs trees to stop topsoil erosion, yet the people desperately need the wood for cooking and heat. The national plan to reforest the land conflicts with the need to cut trees for fuel.

Niger's largest uranium mines are open-pit mines. In open-pit mining, the minerals are removed from the surface rather than by tunneling deep into the earth.

Mining

Uranium is the most valuable product mined in Niger. The nation produces about 4,000 metric tons of processed uranium yearly. There are two major mines and a processing plant that turns the ore into yellowcake uranium. Today, Niger is the world's fourth-largest producer of uranium, but the demand for uranium has decreased dramatically in recent years, and so the price has fallen. France is Niger's largest uranium customer, and the mining company that extracts uranium is French. Twelve percent of Niger's annual national budget comes from earnings on uranium sales.

Niger's largest quarrying product is limestone, with about 23,000,000 metric tons cut from the ground yearly. Limestone is the base material for many types of construction because it can be easily cut into blocks. It can be used for making quicklime, cement, and mortar for gluing bricks together. Limestone is also used in making glass, toothpaste, paper, tiles, and white pigment in paints. Ground limestone gravel makes a good base for asphalt roads.

On a smaller scale, Niger has gold. In 2013, the nation produced 2,376 pounds (1,078 kg) of gold. The Samira Hill gold mine is in the narrow region between the Niger River and the border with Burkina Faso. The mine is fairly new, having opened in 2004.

What Niger Grows, Makes, and Mines

AGRICULTURE (2013)

Millet	2,995,000 metric tons
Cowpeas	1,300,000 metric tons
Sorghum	1,287,000 metric tons

MANUFACTURING (2013)

Food products	6,797,000,000 CFA francs
Paper products, printing	2,604,000,000 CFA francs
Soaps and chemical products	1,625,000,000 CFA francs

MINING (2013)

Limestone	23,200,000 metric tons
Uranium	4,057 metric tons
Gold	1,078 kilograms

Although slavery is outlawed in Niger, international agencies claim there are at least forty-three thousand enslaved people there. By some estimates, the number is as high as eight hundred thousand.

The majority of Nigerien people who are sold are women and children. It is believed that more than ten thousand enslaved children work in Niger's gold mines, stone quarries, or agriculture, or are forced to beg.

Girls, some as young as twelve years old, are sold into fake marriages with men in other countries and then kept as household slaves.

In addition, Niger is a human trafficking route for women and girls sold in neighboring countries. Boys are usually sold for farming and mining work. While the government is making some effort to control human trafficking, it has had little success.

Manufacturing

Niger has very little manufacturing, but what exists takes place mainly in the capital of Niamey. Most products are made for use within the country rather than for export. The most productive manufacturing includes food and food processing, followed by printing and paper products. Niger also makes soaps and chemical products, wood products, and textiles.

There are two standards for measuring manufacturing success: the first is for the entire country and the second is per capita (per person). In 2013, Niger's manufacturing production ranked number 152 in the world, placing it in the bottom third among nations. In per capita production, Niger

Nigeriens who live in the city spend about 40 percent of their family income on food, beverages, and tobacco products. Transportation takes up about 13 percent of the income of urban Nigeriens. Housing and utilities use 10 percent of their income, and clothing costs about the same as utilities.

In the countryside, most Nigeriens live on their own farms. They eat food they produce themselves, and they have no electricity, water, or heating expenses.

Nigeriens who live in cities spend a larger percentage of their money on housing. It may take three salaries to cover the cost of an apartment, utilities, and food.

A truck loaded in Agadez is loaded with onions for export. Onions are a major crop in the Agadez region.

ranked number 201 in the world, which is close to the lowest rank. Nearby countries such as Algeria, Burkina Faso, Chad, Nigeria, Benin, and Libya all produce more goods per person than Niger. Over the past forty years, Niger's manufacturing output has not increased at all while manufacturing in the rest of the world has increased significantly.

Importing and Exporting

Because Niger produces so few goods itself, it must import many products from other countries. Its most valuable import is food and food products. It also imports oil, machinery, chemicals and chemical products, and transportation equipment. Much of these goods are imported from France, China, the Netherlands, and the United States.

Niger's most valuable export item is uranium, which accounts for 75 percent of its exports. Other products exported include gold, onions, and livestock. Most exports are sold to France, Nigeria, the United States, Japan, and Switzerland.

CHAPTER 7

Strong Ties

ASMUN HAS JUST TURNED EIGHTEEN. THIS IS the age when Tuareg males pass from boyhood to adulthood. The family holds a private ceremony to celebrate Asmun becoming an adult. A *marabout* (spiritual leader) blesses both Asmun and the veil he will wear for the rest of his life. All Tuareg men go veiled in public. The veil is a long piece of cotton, measuring 60 to 160 inches (150 to 410 cm) and usually dyed deep blue. The cloth is wrapped around the head to form a turban, with a length used to cover the lower half of the face.

Veiling is a social custom with a number of purposes. On the practical side, the veil keeps blowing sand from reaching the nose and mouth. Spiritually, the veil is thought to prevent evil spirits from entering a man's face. Socially, the veil maintains a Tuareg man's sense of reserve and modesty.

Opposite: **Although a blue veil and blue clothing are traditional for Tuareg men, today other colors are also worn.**

Boys play soccer in Niamey. In 1900, Niamey was home to fewer than 1,000 people. Today, 1.5 million people live in the city and the urban area around it.

Population of Major Cities (2014 est.)

Niamey	774,235
Zinder	191,424
Maradi	163,487
Agadez	124,324

By the Numbers

Niger's population was estimated to be 18,045,729 people in 2015. Taking a census is not an easy job in Niger. Some people are nomadic and are difficult to count. Nearly half of all Nigeriens are under age fifteen. Of those people, only 18.7 percent live in cities. Cities are getting bigger, however, with the urban population growing by 5 percent per year. Increasingly, rural people who can no longer farm because of drought are moving to the cities.

Ethnic Cultures

Niger's population is divided into distinct ethnic groups. For the most part, each group has its own traditional region in the country. The largest group is Hausa, who make up 55 percent of the people. Zarma-Songhais account for 21 percent of Nigeriens. Smaller groups include the Tuareg, the Fulani (or Peul), and the Kanuri-Manga people. In recent years, the population has begun to shift from rural to urban. Members of ethnic groups have begun marrying across cultures and blurring distinct ethnic lines.

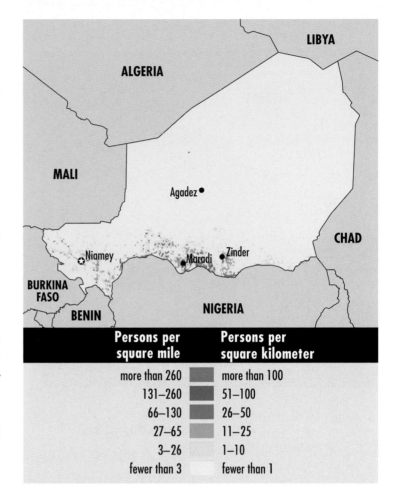

Persons per square mile		Persons per square kilometer
more than 260		more than 100
131–260		51–100
66–130		26–50
27–65		11–25
3–26		1–10
fewer than 3		fewer than 1

Hausa

The Hausas are the largest ethnic group in Niger and dominate the political and economic life of the country. The traditional region of Hausas is the Sahel, and the traditional economy is farming or herding sheep. The people speak the Hausa language, and some who have been educated speak French.

In the past, Hausa society was structured much like a feudal society in Europe. There was a ruler (an emir) who ran a large state. Each village within that state had a noble who acted on the emir's behalf. These nobles maintained order and

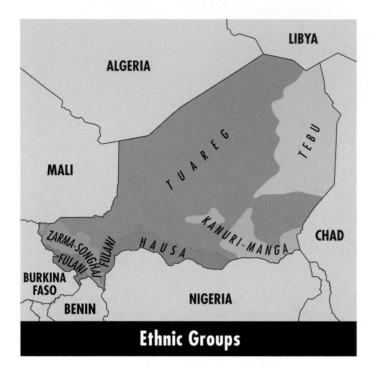

Ethnic Groups

collected taxes for the emir. Times have changed, but in some ways Hausa culture today is similar to older Hausa society.

Hausa people today live in cities, towns, and villages. Hausas who farm live in mud-and-straw huts in villages with the entire household in one home. A farm household has two or more adult males and their families. City dwellers live in walled compounds made of several housing units, and wealthier Hausa live in private homes.

Zarma-Songhai

About 3,300,000 Zarma-Songhais live in Niger, making them the second-largest ethnic group in the country. Traditionally, Zarma-Songhais farm in the southwestern region of Niger. They grow millet, sorghum, and rice for staples, and tomatoes, carrots, lettuce, okra, and potatoes in smaller family kitchen gardens. Usually, only family members work on Zarma-Songhai farms, so families tend to have many children. Boys the ages of six or seven often help with plowing, planting, weeding, and harvesting crops. Girls also help with childcare, pounding millet into flour, and selling food in open markets. The oldest male is the head of the household. The majority of Zarma-Songhais are Muslim.

Ethnic Groups (2015)	
Hausa	55.4%
Zarma-Songhai	21%
Tuareg	9.3%
Fulani or Peul	8.5%
Kanuri-Manga	4.7%
Other	1.2%

*Note: Total does not equal 100 percent because of rounding.

Women and children in the town of Torodi in the southwest. Niger has the highest birth rate in the world, with women having an average of about seven children.

Tuareg

The Tuareg are called the blue men of the Sahara. This nickname comes from the indigo dye that colors their clothes—and their skin—blue. The clothes they wear look bulky, but they are designed to protect the body from the punishing Sahara sun. Clothing is made of cotton and covers the body head to toe.

Women wear long, richly colored dresses, often of blue or purple. Over the dress is a robe. The robe is a long piece of cloth, about 6.5 feet by 16 feet (2 m by 5 m). Women tie the

A Tuareg woman and child. Tuareg women have a higher social status than women in other ethnic groups in the region.

cloth across their shoulders, and then wrap the cloth around the body and over the head. The outer wrap is so well arranged that the dress underneath is not usually seen. Men wear a long cotton shirt over an undershirt and a pair of cotton trousers. The overshirt has long sleeves and drapes nearly to the ankles. All adult men wear veils.

The most valued possession of every Tuareg is a camel. The men of the Aïr region spend nearly five months a year on camel caravans. They travel to Bilma and trade goods for dates and salt. They move from Bilma to Kano, Nigeria, and trade the dates and salt for grain, household goods, spices, cloth, and perfume.

Unlike other Nigerien people, the Tuareg trace their family line through the women. The men are leaders, but the women own the tents, household goods, and herds of goats, sheep, and camels. If a Tuareg husband leaves his wife, he leaves with nothing; his wife keeps everything of value.

Fulani, or Peul

The Fulani, or Peul, people live in several countries in West Africa. They make up the second-largest ethnic group in the region with twenty-five million Fulanis spread across several countries. In Niger, Fulanis make up 8.5 percent of the population. Young Fulanis speak Fulfulde and French, although many of the elderly speak only Fulfulde. This ethnic group is scattered all through Niger's Sahel region. Fulanis are traditionally a nomadic people, but many settle on farms for long periods of

A group of Tuareg men repair a motorcycle. Many Tuareg people use motorcycles when they need to get someplace quickly.

The Wodaabe are a subgroup of the Fulani ethnic group. Wodaabe women adorn themselves with facial scar tattoos, which are considered a sign of beauty.

their lives. The people have a set social system, with four groups or castes. The nobility is the highest, followed by merchants, blacksmiths, and the descendants of slaves. People are born into a caste and remain in that caste throughout their lives.

The most important goal for Fulani society is to own cattle. A person with several cattle is considered wealthy. Once, the group traveled with their cattle searching for fodder. Today, modern technology has reduced the number of people who continue nomadic lifestyles. Most today have settled into towns and villages.

Beauty is highly regarded among Fulanis. A young girl in search of a husband will wear all her jewelry to show her value. Large earrings and multiple ear piercings are common. Women have many tattoos on their bodies, the most obvious being blackish lip color. This comes from using henna or tattoo ink. Women also paint designs on their skin to be more attractive.

Young Fulani males are expected to be brave in the face of danger. One rite of passage used to be for two boys to injure each other with spears, with each boy laughing rather than showing pain. Because many young men died in these ceremonies, the practice has been legally banned.

Niger Naming Systems

Each ethnic group in Niger has its own system for naming its children.

Tuareg: The naming ceremony begins when the infant is six days old. The mother's father and the local spiritual leader choose a name that fits the baby. The women gather to cut the baby's hair and come up with a second name, which will be the name the baby is called within the family.

Hausa: Seven days after a baby is born, the father gathers kola nuts to give to family and friends. Males are usually named after Islamic prophets. Girls are given traditional Hausa women's names.

Fulani: A Fulani newborn is named on its seventh day after birth. The naming of the first-born child is accompanied by a large celebration.

Kanuri-Manga

There are 538,000 Kanuri-Manga living in Niger. Most live in a small area of the Sahel slightly east of Zinder and bordering on Nigeria. Most Kanuris are farmers, and many have a second job during the dry season. Common crops on Kanuri farms include sorghum, maize, and groundnuts. Many Kanuri farmers also raise sheep or goats. A sign of wealth and status among the Kanuri people is owning a horse.

Kanuri social status also comes from the size of a household, which consists of the core family, workers, and relatives who live with or work for the family. Households follow the direc-

Kanuri men load salt pillars onto camels. The Kanuri people have long been involved in salt processing and trade.

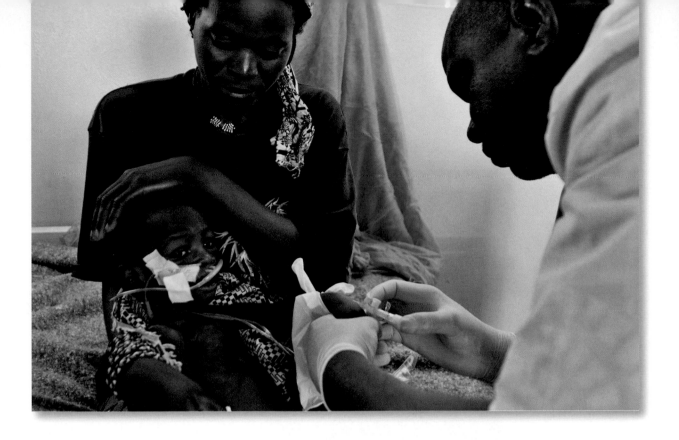

tions set down by the father. Often, young men are loaned out to a neighboring family for work or to defend the family.

Health Care

Simply surviving can be a struggle in Niger. Access to adequate health care and food are frequent problems. Across the country, there is one doctor for every forty thousand people. This statistic is deceiving, however, since most doctors work in cities, and most Nigeriens live in rural areas. Many Nigeriens never see a trained medical doctor.

One child in every six dies before reaching five years old. Nigeriens also have one of the lowest life expectancies of any country in the world, with people expected to live just fifty-nine years.

A Nigerien doctor treats an ill child. In Niger, the percentage of infants and young children who die has decreased in recent years as the government has tried to make health care more available and improve the vaccination rate.

A Nigerien woman separates grain from its husks. Food shortages caused by drought are a frequent problem in Niger.

The high death rate is related to both health care and the food supply. Two-thirds of the population lives in poverty, which means many families go hungry. In 2010, 17 percent of Niger's children suffered from malnutrition. Lack of food equals lack of vitamins, protein, and minerals needed for good health. Children who do not eat well are more prone to diseases. Lack of clean drinking water means exposure to cholera, typhus, and other deadly diseases.

Languages

Niger's major ethnic groups, its French colonial history, and its Muslim heritage have all influenced the languages of its people. The official national languages of Niger are French and Hausa. Most ethnic groups speak their own language at home and among their group. Nigeriens involved in trade, travel, or business usually speak their native language, plus French and Hausa. The most common languages heard in Niger are Hausa and Zarma. There are, however, more than twenty languages or versions of languages spoken in Niger.

Some of these languages are spoken by millions of people. Other languages are confined to small regions or villages with as few as three thousand speakers.

Although French is the national language of Niger, French speakers are in the minority. Many more people speak Hausa or Zarma. French is spoken by many people around the world and is considered the language of diplomacy. Many international organizations rely on French as a working language between countries where different languages are spoken. French is an official language in more than two dozen countries around the world,

Classes in most schools in Niger are taught in the French language.

including Niger's neighbors Benin, Burkina Faso, Cameroon, Ivory Coast, and Chad. For Nigeriens, French makes it easier for a Hausa person to speak to a Tuareg or for a Fulani person to speak to a Zarma. It allows the country to do business with France, Switzerland, Burkina Faso, and many other nations.

Hausa is the native language of more than thirty-nine million people, including both Nigeriens and Nigerians. Another fifteen million people speak Hausa as a second language. In the seventeenth century, people wrote Hausa using an Arabic writing system called *ajami*. Ajami does not represent specific letters. There is no defined spelling of words, since the language was passed down mainly from parent to child. Today, Hausa is written in *boko*, which is an alphabet like the one used in English, French, or Latin.

Zarma is the second most-widely spoken language in Niger. The Zarma and the Songhai people do not speak the exact same language, but the two are very similar. Zarma-Songhai speakers live in southwestern Niger in the area around Niamey. These languages are also spoken in Mali, Burkina Faso, and Benin.

The Fulani, or Peul, people speak Fulfulde. Across West Africa, about fifteen million people speak this language, although it is not one of the more common languages in Niger. This language can be written in both ajami script and Latin letters.

The Tuareg speak Tamasheq, which has its own alphabet, called *tifinagh*. The Tuareg language is one of a family of Berber languages. Tamasheq is also spoken in Tunisia, Morocco, Algeria, and Libya. Tuareg mothers are expected to teach their children how to read and write Tamasheq.

The Qur'an, the holy book of Islam, is written in Arabic. Muslim children learn to read Arabic so they can read the Qur'an in its original language. In some Nigerien cities, religious leaders teach Arabic at the local mosques. The television station broadcasts news in Arabic daily.

With so many languages spoken within its borders, the government of Niger needs to find ways to communicate with everyone. Though French is the official language, Nigeriens are not forced to speak French or to give up their ethnic languages. The Office of Radio and Television of Niger produces broadcasts for radio and television. Télé Sahel, the television station, provides news in Hausa, Zarma, Tamasheq, Fulfulde, Kanouri, Toubou, and other languages. Most other programs are in French. The radio station, La Voix du Sahel, provides government-sponsored broadcasts in all major languages.

A Hausa boy holds a board with passages from the Qur'an at a mosque in Zinder. At Islamic schools, children memorize parts of the Qur'an.

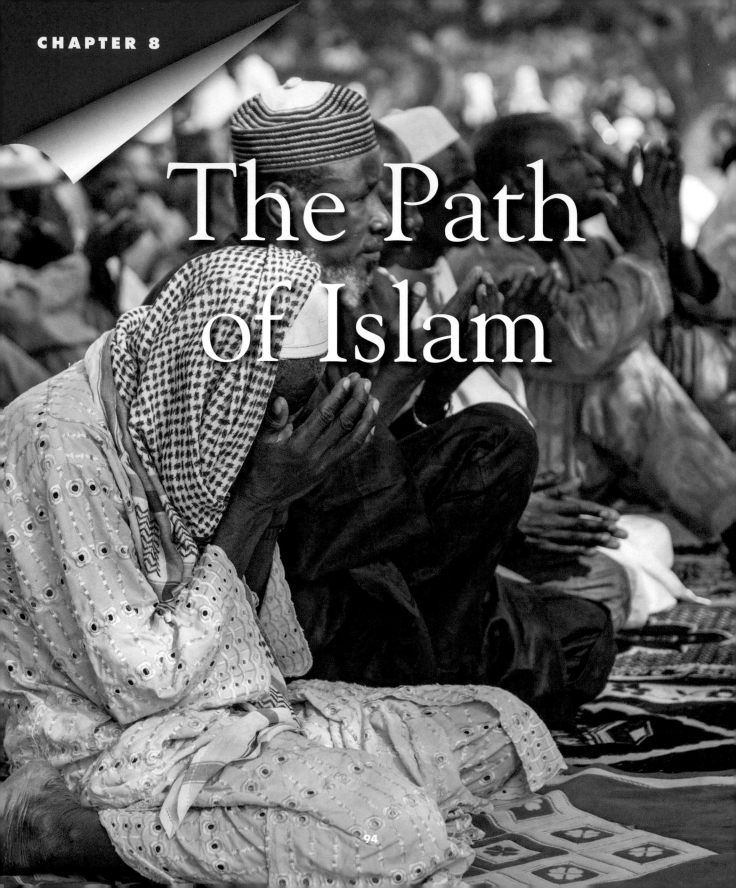

CHAPTER 8

The Path of Islam

TAMILA RISES BEFORE DAWN. SHE WASHES HER HANDS and face, then kneels and says her first prayers of the day. She lays a fire among the cooking stones in front of the family tent. She puts a large pot of millet, dates, and water on the fire to cook. When the sun rises, she will pray again. Tamila prays inside the family tent. Her husband, Iken, joins the men in prayers. Men and women do not pray together.

Tamila and Iken are Tuareg. They are Muslim, but the Tuareg have adjusted the teachings of Islam to fit their lives. They have added traditional Tuareg beliefs to blend in with being Muslim. In many places, Muslim women wear veils over their heads in public. Among the Tuareg, men veil their faces as a sign of manhood.

Opposite: **Nigeriens pray during a festival marking the end of Ramadan, the holiest time of the year for Muslims.**

An imam, or Muslim religious leader, speaks to a group of worshipers in Agadez at the end of Ramadan.

Yet, like other Muslims, the Tuareg pray five times daily as required by the Qur'an. They celebrate the Prophet Muhammad's birthday, and they fast, or do not eat, during the daylight hours in the holy month of Ramadan. In these ways, they are like most people in Niger, where Muslims make up about 98 percent of all citizens.

Following the Prophet

Muslims believe that in 610 CE, God began revealing messages to a man named Muhammad, in Mecca, a city now in Saudi Arabia. According to Islam, Muhammad continued to receive messages from God for twenty-two years. These messages were compiled to form the Qur'an, the basis of Islam.

A framework called the five pillars of Islam is considered the basis of Muslim life. The first pillar is the testimony of faith, which states "There is no god but God, and Muhammad is the messenger of God."

The second pillar says that Muslims are supposed to pray five times daily. Prayer is considered a direct link between those who pray and Allah, the Arabic word for "God." In cities, a person called a muezzin announces when it is time to pray. Some men go to a mosque to pray, but it is not necessary. Prayer can be done from the home, in an open field, or on a sand dune.

The third pillar of Islam is to give help to those who are less fortunate. Called *zakat*, this required giving purifies the possessions of the giver. Usually a set percentage of a person's earnings is pledged for zakat.

The fourth pillar of faith is fasting during Ramadan. During this month, Muslims do not eat or drink from sunup to sundown. It is a time to pray and purify the soul. Each day after sundown during Ramadan, Muslims feast, spend time with family and friends, and pray. At the end of Ramadan, the celebration of Eid al-Fitr breaks the fast.

Mosques typically include a tower, called a minaret, from which the call to prayer is broadcast, indicating that it is time for Muslims to pray. The 89-foot (27 m) minaret at the Grand Mosque in Agadez is the world's tallest minaret made of mud bricks.

The final pillar of Islam is that every Muslim should make a pilgrimage, called *hajj*, to Mecca at least once. This requirement is for those in good health and with sufficient money to make the journey.

Muslim Holidays

Most religious holidays in Niger follow the Islamic calendar. This calendar is eleven days shorter than the Gregorian calendar used in the United States, so Muslim holidays fall on different dates each year according to the Gregorian calendar.

Every year millions of pilgrims gather in Mecca, Saudi Arabia, for the hajj. During the hajj, which lasts five days, pilgrims wear white robes and perform a series of rituals.

Muharram, the first month of the Islamic calendar, is a sacred month. Traditionally, it was against Islamic beliefs to go to war during Muharram.

Korité, also called Eid al-Fitr, celebrates the end of Ramadan. Family members get together and enjoy a feast. Part of the feast is given to those who are less fortunate. Korité is a public holiday in Niger, as well as a religious event.

Lailatul-Qadr honors the Revelation of the Qur'an. On this night, Muslims celebrate the word of the Qur'an. It is a time when sins are said to be erased.

Tabaski, known in other regions as Eid al-Adha, is a festival that honors the sacrifice of Abraham. It is said that God

Tuareg men perform a dance celebrating Islamic New Year.

Some Hausas follow a traditional religion called Bori. In this religion, people sometimes dance until they are said to be possessed by a spirit and go into a trance.

asked Abraham to sacrifice his son Ishmael. Abraham was willing to do so for God. He lifted his blade, and God replaced Ishmael with a sheep. Thus, for Tabaski a sheep is slaughtered, and family and friends share the roast mutton.

Mouloud honors the birth of the Prophet Muhammad. The celebration includes a feast of roast mutton. There are also horse or camel races, and families get together.

Other Religions

Many Nigeriens have two belief systems. For example, people may be Muslim, but also have beliefs that tie them to the old traditions. Many Nigeriens did not begin to follow Islam until the twentieth century. In some cases, Nigeriens follow Islam with some modifications. In most of Niger, women are not expected to veil their faces, and women are allowed to own and inherit property.

A small percentage of Nigeriens follow other religions. A belief in animism occurs among both Zarma-Songhai and Hausa people. Followers of animism make offerings to the spirits. Ritual dancing is believed to keep the spirits under control and the followers healthy. Spirits are thought to be able to possess the body or cause illness. Animists also believe spirits can provide the cure for such illnesses. Hausa animists depend on the assistance of priests or priestesses. Among Zarma-Songhais, it is common to ask praise singers and spirit priests to help people through troubled times.

Some Nigeriens in cities practice Christian religions. Roman Catholicism and Protestant faiths came to Niger with the French. Today, Christian missionaries are common in Niger.

A Christian minister leads a service in Niamey. More than fifty thousand Nigeriens are Christian.

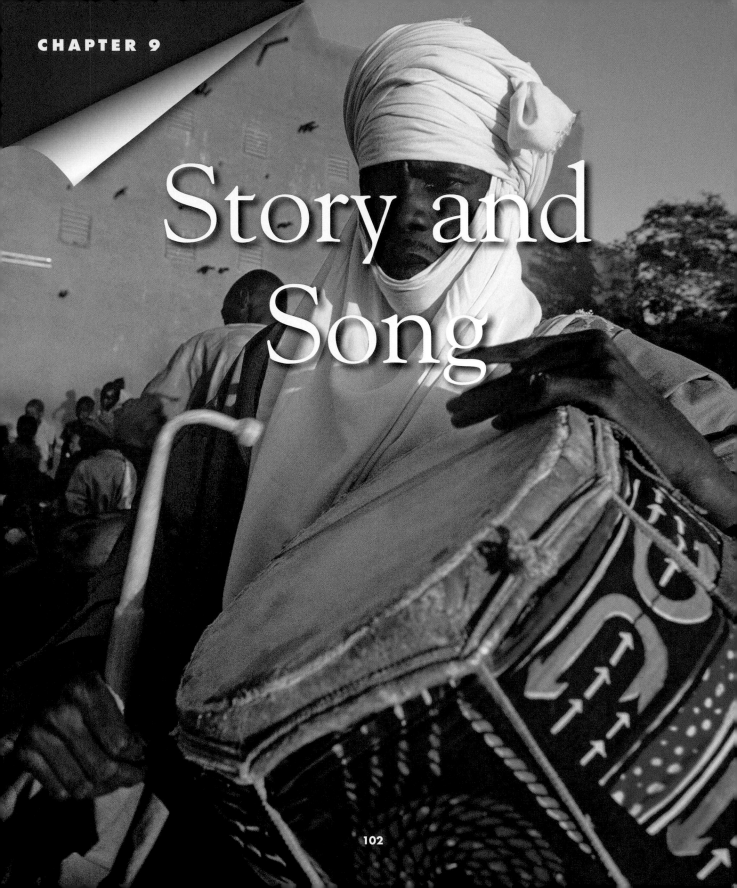

CHAPTER 9

Story and Song

DJIBO BADJÉ SITS AT A CAMPFIRE WITH A GROUP OF Zarma teens. To most people in Niamey, Djibo is the greatest Zarma historian alive today. He tells tales of Zarma heroes from many years ago. Djibo is a *jasare*, a storyteller who recalls the history and family lines of the Zarma people going back many generations. The stories do not deal with just one or two rulers or battles. Djibo knows the family trees of nearly three hundred Zarma chiefdoms, and about the bravery of the Zarma people. He learned these stories from his father, who was also a jasare. His father also taught him how to play the *moolo*, a lute-like instrument played only by jasare.

Storytelling is a Nigerien tradition that is fulfilled by griots (storytellers) and jasare (historians). The tales pass from father to son, and the lessons begin at an early age. Djibo knows that his gift will not pass down to the next generation. His sons are not interested in memorizing tales of people long

Opposite: **Drumming plays a role in most Nigerien celebrations.**

Tuareg women make a drum by wrapping a hide over the base and then securing it tightly with a rope.

dead. Yet, the stories and history are part of Niger's oral tradition. In the past, the history and genealogy had never been written down or recorded. Djibo, the last of his line, worked with a Swiss social scientist to preserve this unique knowledge for generations to come.

Tell Me a Story

A griot is a storyteller, and Nigeriens admire those who can tell a good tale. Griots carry on the oral tradition of sharing folktales, reciting poetry, recalling history, and relating proverbs. Through song, they tell the stories of past glory from legends, epic poems, and lengthy tales. Griots often accompany themselves with a three-stringed lute, and sometimes other musicians accompany them.

Music

Music is as much a part of Niger's culture as storytelling. Traditional instruments include the *algaita*, *kakaki*, *kukkuma*, and *xalam*. An algaita is a wind instrument that produces rich sounds similar to an oboe. It has a large bell, much like a trumpet, and finger holes for playing specific notes. Like the algaita, the kakaki is a long wind instrument. Measuring as long as 13 feet (4 m), the kakaki is the classic instrument of the Hausa people. It is heard only at royal ceremonies when it is played for a king or other leader.

Another Hausa instrument is the kukkuma, a small fiddle. For many griots, the instrument of choice is the *kora*, a

The kakaki is made from brass or tin. Only men play this instrument.

twenty-one-string lute that sounds much like a harp. It takes years to learn these instruments. The xalam, another stringed instrument, is similar to a banjo.

In addition to wind and string instruments, Nigerien musicians play a variety of drums. Wind and stringed instruments provide the melody, but hand drums provide the rhythm. No

The *imzad* is a single-stringed instrument played only by Tuareg women. It is played to accompany poems and stories about past adventures or heroes.

dance is held without at least one drummer pounding out the beat to which feet tap and hips sway.

Popular groups combine ancient rhythms with modern music styles. Well-known musicians include Ismaël Lô and Zara Moussa. They produce music that is sold worldwide. Mdou Moctar is a singer, a songwriter, and an actor.

Folk Arts

Each of Niger's ethnic groups has a long tradition of folk arts. Hausa people paint patterns on the outside of their homes, which are rectangular and made from earthen bricks. When the flat fronts of the buildings are painted in interesting geometric patterns, they look like bright, colorful, and dramatic patchwork quilts. Many of the patterns are borrowed from Islamic art, and every house's art is distinctive.

Tuareg artisans make valuable leatherwork and jewelry. Their leather products include saddles, belts, camel bags, and water containers. The saddles are for camels, and the

During ceremonies, Wodaabe men wear headdresses adorned with ostrich feathers. The feathers are intended to make them appear more appealing to women.

water containers are made from goatskin. The jewelry is usually silver and heavily influenced by Islamic designs. The artisans design earrings, rings, anklets, and medallions. Their most significant product is the Agadez silver cross, called the *tenegheit*.

Village artisans make pots, baskets, and handwoven cloth. Vegetable dyes add yellows, browns, and reds to village weaving. Reeds make excellent floor mats, while hand-spun wool is ideal for blankets.

Fulani men and women decorate their bodies with makeup, tattoos, feathers, and beads. In order to make themselves more attractive, they paint their lips blue or black, add ornate painted designs to the skin, and hang multiple layers of beads around their necks. Men's headdresses are adorned with feathers. Women wear rings through their noses, long earrings, and row upon row of braids.

Sports

Traditional wrestling draws more fans than any other sport in Niger. Men and women, young and old, Nigeriens support their favorites, bet on outcomes, and praise the victors. In traditional wrestling, matches are held outdoors, in large rings marked in the sand. The competitors begin in a standing position. The winner is the first person to force his opponent to touch the ground with a part of the body other than a hand or foot. Each year, the National Championship of Traditional Wrestling arranges matches. The event begins with the opening prayer, a series of praise poems, and greetings to contestants and fans. After the final match, the winner is declared a national hero.

Nigerien Dan Lele (right) throws a competitor to the ground in a traditional wrestling match. The sport is popular throughout West Africa.

During the rest of the year, fans flock to horse races, camel races, and team sports. Soccer is the most popular team sport. Some Nigeriens also play rugby. Both rugby and soccer are played on the amateur and professional levels.

Performing Arts and Film

Every Nigerien ethnic group has traditional dances that are performed for courting a prospective bride or groom, celebrating a wedding, or mourning the death of a friend or family member. One traditional dance is called the *tam-tam*. Drummers play, young women dance, and the viewers are entertained. Part of the entertainment includes tossing coins to the ground to pay the musicians.

In Niamey, there is a small theater program that started more than thirty years ago. The founder, Yazi Dogo, has spent his life presenting comedies and educational productions to entertain Niger's youth. His work is shown at the Oumarou Ganda Arts Center, which serves as a recreation center for young and old.

The arts center is named for one of Niger's best-known directors and actors. Ganda appeared in films during the 1960s and 1970s. His films include *Cabascabo*, *Le Wazzou Polygame*, and *L'Exilé*. *Cabascabo* is a film about a young soldier in Indochina who sees his friends die in battle. The film mirrors Ganda's life. *L'Exilé* retells a classic African folktale. Ganda's works were part of a golden age of moviemaking in Niger.

Although the Nigerien movie business has slowed, new movies are still being produced. In 2014, the first Tuareg movie, *Akounak Teggdalit Taha Tazoughai*, debuted. The story of a struggling Tuareg musician, it is based on *Purple Rain*, a 1984 movie that starred the American musician Prince. Tamasheq, the language of the Tuareg, has no word for *purple*, however, so the film's title translates as "rain the color of blue with a little red in it." The movie, set in Agadez, features one of Niger's most popular musicians, Mdou Moctar.

A Nigerien woman dances at a wedding party.

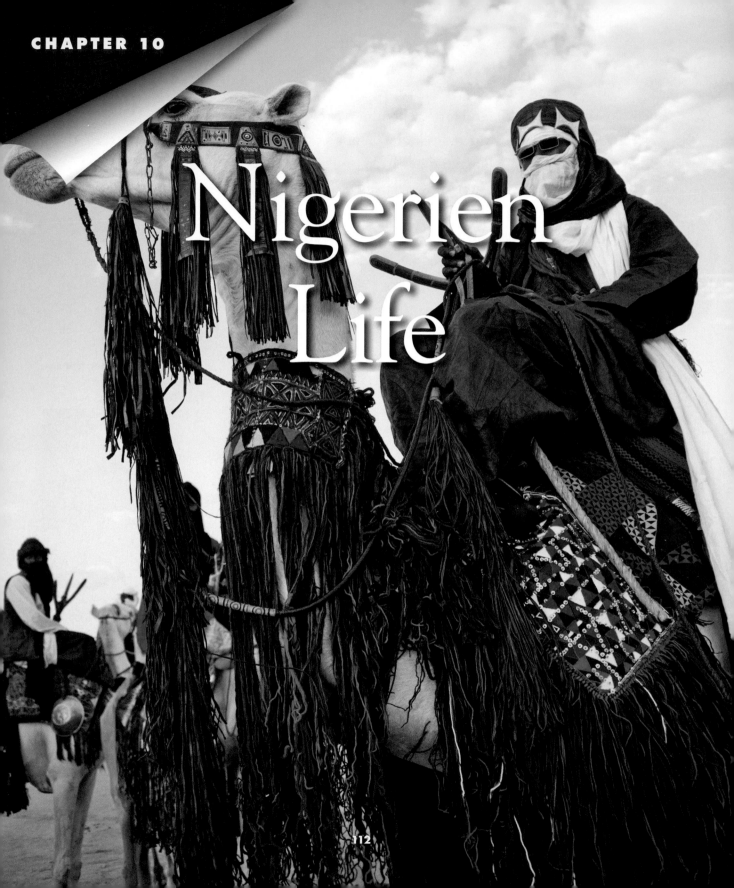

CHAPTER 10

Nigerien Life

T IS LATE SEPTEMBER, AND HUNDREDS OF TUAREG and other nomadic people gather in In-Gall, a town in northern Niger. The rains have ended for this year. Now, it is time to celebrate, heal, and prepare for the dry months to come. Called *Cure Salée*, or salt cure, it is a time for rest, as well as a time for young men and women to try to attract a spouse.

Tents pop up around the outskirts of In-Gall. Herders make sure their cattle, goats, and sheep are refreshed and healthy. The livestock enjoy water and salt licks. The sick meet with local healers and try to overcome illness. Men sit around fires and talk about trade, livestock, and their riding skills. Women gather around cook fires and discuss children, the year's harvest, and family matters.

During the festival, Tuareg men show off their riding skills in a camel parade and exhibit their dancing and music skills for eligible women. There are camel races during the day, and music and dancing at night.

Opposite: **A Tuareg competes in a camel-riding competition at the Cure Salée.**

Wodaabe men adorn themselves with makeup during the Cure Salée. The makeup is intended to highlight the whiteness of the eyes and teeth, signs of beauty in their culture.

Meanwhile, another nomadic group—the Wodaabe, who belong to the Fulani ethnic group—celebrates its own courtship rituals. The Wodaabe paint their faces, don their best clothing, and enhance their appearance with beads and feathers. The young women watch the men carefully.

Although Cure Salée officially lasts three days, the actual event may go on for weeks. During this time, artisans trade goods, and livestock is examined and bought or sold. The dry months ahead will be hard. The clans will go their separate ways, and many people will not see each other until the following September. Tents are taken down, and goods packed up. Friends bid farewell for another year, when they will meet again at In-Gall's salt pots.

Social Status and Castes

In villages, there is a distinct noble class and an equally distinct lower class. In cities, status depends more on money. The
upper class earns more, owns more, and enjoys more power.
The lower class in cities is made up of the poor. A change
is happening in the status of people in the cities: A growing

**Women shop for pots
at a Nigerien market.**

In rural Niger, it is usually considered the women's job to fetch water each day. In some parts of the country, this can take hours.

middle class is emerging as shopkeepers and service providers become more successful.

One thing that is slow to change is the status of women in Niger. Across the country, a girl grows up in her father's home and moves from there to her husband's home. Despite efforts to include women in the political process and appoint women to high offices, this does not often occur. Women are allowed to vote, but in many cases, their husbands tell them which candidate to vote for.

In rural areas, women work hard and demands on them are heavy. Men travel, leaving the women to take care of the children, collect firewood, crush grain, cook, tend crops, fetch water, and deal with the everyday work of scratching out a living. Some women never leave the home. They are expected to remain in it at all times, and when they do go out, they must be accompanied by their older children. Older women can go out more because they are not expected to care for children. One of the most respected avenues open to rural women is to become an herbal healer.

Life at Home

Most Nigerien people live closely within family groups. The average household has four to six people living in one home. Homes are not large. They are also not easily available. The

A Tuareg healer sorts medicinal herbs. She uses leaves, roots, and barks to cure ailments.

The village of Tahoua, in southwestern Niger, features typical Hausa architecture. People live in square houses built of mud bricks and store grain in large oval buildings.

government has tried to increase the number of abodes, but most Nigeriens in cities do not earn enough money to buy one.

Most rural and many urban homes have no electricity. For those with electricity, the service is irregular. Many Nigeriens have no running water or indoor plumbing. Women line up at the local well every day and haul a day's worth of water home.

People in Niger live in several different types of homes. Nomadic groups live in tents so they can move easily. The Tuareg live in covered tents. Fulanis use small, collapsible huts that have roofs made of straw mats. Both Tuareg and Fulani dwellings can be packed up in a minimal amount of time.

People who live in villages have more permanent huts. In cities and towns, family homes are usually made of clay or concrete. The roofs of clay houses are sometimes tiled, but are more often made of straw mats or wood coated in clay. In cities and towns, some homes have a bathroom, while in rural homes people bathe from bowls or pails.

Parents and children live in the same home and may all sleep in the same room. Women and children live in the same home as their husbands and fathers, but men and women live separate lives. The men eat together, visit with friends, play cards, and travel with their work. Women are restricted to their homes by children and tradition. In rural areas, it would be unusual to see a woman away from her home, though some routinely travel to visit relatives or seek the services of healers.

Three Cups of Tea

Whenever people visit someone's home among the Tuareg, the polite thing for the host to do is offer tea. Tea is considered the "friend of conversation." The kettle is put on the fire. Tea is spooned into the pot, followed by water and sugar. While the tea brews, friends share news about the weather, crops, children, and livestock. For the guest, it is rude to leave before drinking three cups of tea. That covers just about the amount of time it takes to share all the best gossip. Young men everywhere have now adopted the practice of drinking tea among themselves.

Men relax over a game of cards in Agadez.

Free Time

While few people in Niger can afford to entertain on a grand scale, everyone can spare time for a visit. Women chat over a bowl of millet as they pound the grain into flour. One woman talks with another as they take time to braid hair or apply henna designs to the palms of hands or the soles of feet. While cooking, sweeping, or working the fields, young women sing and dance. In villages, electricity is rare, with only one in four people having reliable electric service. Clever viewers rig up televisions to car batteries to enjoy news and sports events. French television shows keep people inside when nights grow chilly. Men who own televisions enjoy visits from male friends who want to share a night's viewing.

In the cities, men go to clubs or to the movies. Films draw crowds to outdoor movie theaters, where viewers gather for the latest romance or martial arts blockbuster.

Men in cities and villages spend time together over tea. When time allows, they play *belote* or *dilli*. Belote is a French card game that uses a thirty-two-card deck. Dilli is a gambling game. It is played with palm nuts and sticks, and is somewhat like backgammon without the board.

Marriage

Dating is not common in Niger. Young women in villages meet young men at traditional events or at weddings. Among nomadic groups, teenage girls look for a husband at the Cure Salée. For the most part, parents arrange marriages. Brides and grooms can refuse their parents' choice of spouse, but few people marry without their parents' approval. Many young people whose first marriage was arranged by their parents end up divorcing to make a "marriage of love." There is no stigma attached to divorce. It is not considered unusual for a woman to have been married four or five times.

In urban areas, the traditional custom of parents choosing a husband or wife is slowly changing. Young people are beginning to be allowed more freedom in choosing a spouse. Young people meet and get to know each other. Young men invite women to restaurants, for walks, or for picnics by the river, and sometimes they pay young women a visit at their home. Not all families permit these activities, however.

For both rural and urban people, marriage is expected. In

Greeting the World

According to Nigerien custom, after a baby is born, neither the mother nor child leaves the house for forty days. This is more common in rural villages than in cities.

When the baby is seven days old, the local religious leader, the *marabout*, holds a naming ceremony. The mother is given soap and money. The new mother receives all her friends and acquaintances in her room. These visits last all day.

Men gather separately from the women, outside the compound early in the morning. The marabout says prayers for the baby's health. A ram is slaughtered, roasted, and served to guests for a midday meal along with dates and millet. The baby's name is announced, and the father passes out kola nuts as part of the celebration.

When it is finally time to leave the house, the mother dresses in her best clothes. Her husband, family, and friends give her presents.

rural areas, girls as young as seven often have marriages arranged to take place when they are older. Four out of five girls marry by age eighteen. The legal age for marriage is fifteen, although rural communities do not always follow the law, and some girls marry at twelve. It is rare to find a rural woman in her twenties who is not already married. Men, too, are expected to marry and father children. A man without children is not entitled to the same respect as heads of households.

Young men marry between the ages of eighteen and twenty-five. It is legal for men to have as many as four wives at a time. Women are limited to only one husband at a time. Today, young men are moving away from having more than one wife. One reason is the expense. A husband has to provide a home for each of his wives. It is expensive to feed, house, clothe, and educate the children of four wives. In addition, many young men speak of marrying for love and wish to have only one wife.

A married couple becomes part of the husband's family. They live with or next to the husband's parents. If they have

a separate home, it is in the same compound as the parents' home. In cities, it is more common for married couples to live away from the husband's parents. One reason is the cost of living in cities. It may be hard for a young couple to afford to live close to the husband's parents' home.

Children at a school in Niamey. In Niger, children start school at age seven.

At School

Childhood does not last long in rural Niger. At age seven, children take on adult responsibilities. Boys learn how to handle livestock, cut fodder, and sell goods. Girls help their mothers and learn how to cook, clean, sew clothing, weave cloth, farm, and harvest crops.

Although public education is free, many families cannot afford to send their children to school because they are needed to work on the family farm. Still, a growing number of Nigerien children attend school. Today, more than half of Niger's children go to school, even in rural areas. By middle school, attendance drops significantly, especially for girls, who are expected to help at home and often earn money as well.

In Niger, classes are taught in French, which creates problems for children who may speak Hausa, Zarma, or Tamasheq as their native language. A few schools teach in a local ethnic language, and the Tuareg usually teach their children at home. There are also bilingual schools in Arabic and French that combine the modern secular curriculum in French with Islamic education in Arabic.

Niger has several schools of higher education. Abdou Moumouni University in Niamey has an enrollment of just over

A woman buys yams at a market in Niamey. A wide variety of fruits and vegetables is available in southern Niger.

thirteen thousand. It includes a teacher training college, three research institutes, and a school of agriculture. The university has branch campuses in Maradi, Zinder, and Tahoua. The Islamic University of Niger, located in Say, south of Niamey, offers courses in Arabic, Islamic studies, Sharia law, science and technology, economics, and agriculture. The Islamic University also has a woman's college for Islamic Studies and Arabic Language. Less than 1 percent of Nigeriens of college age are enrolled in a university. There are few female students because most college-aged girls are already married.

What's to Eat?

In rural areas, people live on a subsistence diet of millet, sorghum, beans, and vegetables. Men and women work the millet and sorghum fields, plowing, sowing seed, and harvesting. They pound millet into coarse flour, which is used to make porridge, flatbreads, and a drink that is served sweet or sour. Sorghum is also grown and eaten as a type of flour. Sorghum grain can be heated in oil and popped like corn. Most people also keep a goat, sheep, or zebu for milk, and raise chickens.

In the local markets, women trade extra vegetables to supplement the family diet. Common items on offer include chili peppers, onions, mangoes, dates, oranges, bananas, melons, pomegranates, and kola nuts. People grow okra, peanuts, and tomatoes. During the cold season, kitchen gardens grow yams, potatoes, carrots, and lettuce. Coconuts and sugarcane are popular snacks.

The most common meat is goat, although it is usually kept

Mango Salad

Mangoes are a special treat in Niger. Here is a delicious salad that can be made from mangoes. Have an adult help you.

Ingredients

2 mangoes	1 cup orange juice
½ fresh pineapple	4 large lettuce leaves
½ cup lemon juice	4 strawberries

Directions

Peel and cube the mangoes. Skin, core, and cube the ripe pineapple. Put cubed fruit in a bowl. Add the lemon and orange juice. Mix gently to combine. Peel four large leaves off a head of lettuce. Wash well and dry on paper towel. Each leaf will be used as a small bowl for the fruit. Arrange the fruit in each lettuce cup. Garnish each with a strawberry.

for special occasions. A goat is more valuable for giving milk throughout the year than for a few meals of roast or stewed meat. When meat is eaten, it is grilled as kebabs and heavily spiced or added to the sauce that is poured on the millet, corn, or rice dish that is eaten in the evening. No meat goes to waste. Any leftover pieces are dried and made into goat or sheep jerky.

Dealing with Death

Muslim custom requires that when a person dies, the body be buried the same day or the following day at the latest. The mourning period is a time of prayer. A local religious figure leads prayers and chanting, speaking the final prayers over the deceased.

The body is washed and wrapped in a white cotton shroud and is placed on straw mats. Only men go to the burial. Prayers are said over the body, which is then laid in the grave. Following the burial, people visit the home of the family of the deceased. The men stay in one area and the women stay in another, separate from the men.

Women whose husbands die remain in mourning for three or four months. During that time they cannot eat with the rest of the family and should remain at home.

For most people, mourning the dead lasts forty days. Friends and family visit the home. On the last day of the mourning period, friends arrive early at the home. This last day is for family to enjoy the sweet among the sorrow. Prayers are said. Dates, other fruit, and bean cakes are served. The clothes of the deceased are given to cousins and other people.

Through life's struggles, the people of Niger support one another. They provide each other love, companionship, and solace as they carry on their day-to-day lives.

A group of women walking in Maradi. About 80 percent of Nigerien women are married by the time they are eighteen.

Timeline

NIGER HISTORY

French officers Paul Voulet and Julien Chanoine lead a violent expedition across Niger, killing thousands.	**1898–1899**
Niger becomes part of French West Africa; Zinder is made capital of the Niger territory.	**1922**
Niamey becomes the capital of Niger.	**1926**
The First Republic of Niger is founded; Hamani Diori becomes the first president.	**1960**
Mining uranium becomes a moneymaker for Niger.	**1968**
Seyni Kountché takes power in a military coup.	**1974**
Mahamane Ousmane is elected president.	**1993**
Ousmane is ousted in a coup.	**1996**
Mamadou Tandja is elected president.	**1999**
Mahamadou Issoufou becomes president; Brigi Rafini becomes prime minister.	**2011**
The radical Islamic group Boko Haram raids Nigerien villages.	**2015**

WORLD HISTORY

1914	World War I begins.
1917	The Bolshevik Revolution brings communism to Russia.
1929	A worldwide economic depression begins.
1939	World War II begins.
1945	World War II ends.
1969	Humans land on the Moon.
1975	The Vietnam War ends.
1989	The Berlin Wall is torn down as communism crumbles in Eastern Europe.
1991	The Soviet Union breaks into separate states.
2001	Terrorists attack the World Trade Center in New York City and the Pentagon near Washington, D.C.
2004	A tsunami in the Indian Ocean destroys coastlines in Africa, India, and Southeast Asia.
2008	The United States elects its first African American president.

Fast Facts

Official name: Republic of Niger

Capital: Niamey

Official languages: French, Hausa, Zarma, Fulfulde, Kanuri, Arabic, Gurma, and Tebu

Agadez

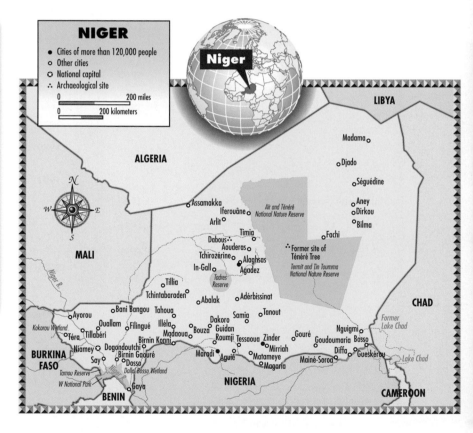

NIGER

- Cities of more than 120,000 people
- Other cities
- National capital
- Archaeological site

0   200 miles
0   200 kilometers

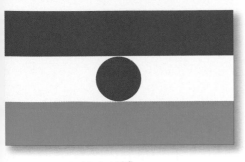

National flag

National anthem: "La Nigérienne" ("The Nigerien")

Type of government: Republic

Head of state: President

Head of government: Prime minister

Area: 489,678 square miles (1,267,000 sq km)

Highest elevation: Mount Idoûkâl-n-Taghès, 6,634 feet (2,022 m) above sea level

Lowest elevation: Niger River (at the Nigerian border), 656 feet (200 m) above sea level

Latitude and longitude of geographic center: 16°00' N, 8°00' E

Largest desert: Sahara

Longest river: Niger River, 342 miles (550 km) in Niger; total length of 2,600 miles (4,180 km)

Largest oasis: Timia

Average high temperature: In Niamey, 106°F (41°C) in April; 91°F (33°C) in August

Average low temperature: In Niamey, 80°F (27°C) in April; 74°F (23°C) in August

Äir Mountains

Grand Mosque of Agadez

Currency

National population (2015 est.): 18,045,729

Population of major cities (2014 est.):

Niamey	774,235
Zinder	191,424
Maradi	163,487
Agadez	124,324

Population distribution:

Urban	18.7%
Rural	81.3%

Landmarks:
- ▶ *Aïr and Ténéré National Nature Reserve*
- ▶ *Dabous petroglyphs*, Ténéré Desert
- ▶ *Grand Mosque*, Agadez
- ▶ *National Museum of Niger*, Niamey
- ▶ *Sultan's Palace*, Zinder

Economy: Uranium mining is an important part of the Nigerien economy. Oil, cement, bricks, soap, textiles, food processing, and chemicals are also part of the Nigerien economy. Crops grown in Niger include millet, sorghum, cassava, and rice. Livestock farmed include cattle, sheep, goats, donkeys, camels, and poultry.

Currency: West African franc (CFA franc). In 2016, 579.5 CFA francs equaled US$1.00.

System of weights and measures: Metric system

Literacy rate (2015): 19.1%

Schoolgirl

Hamani Diori

Hausa words and phrases:

Sannu	Hello
Don Allah	Please
Na gode	Thank you
Ina farin cikin haduwa da kai	Pleased to meet you
Kana jin ingilishi?	Do you speak English?
Sunana…	My name is…
Barka da yamma	Good evening
Sai sannu	Good-bye

Prominent Nigeriens:

Idris Alawma (ca. 1542–ca. 1619)
Bornu leader

Djibo Badjé (1938–)
Griot

Issaka Daborg (1940–)
Olympic boxer

Hamani Diori (1916–1989)
First president of Niger

Yazi Dogo (ca. 1940–)
Founder of a theater group

Oumarou Ganda (1935–1981)
Movie actor

Sarraounia Mangou (?–?)
Hausa queen who fought French colonial troops

Brigi Rafini (1953–)
Prime minister

To Find Out More

Books

▶ Barnes, Trevor. *Islam*. New York: Kingfisher, 2013.

▶ Cushman, Amanda. *Zarma Folktales of Niger*. Niantic, CT: Quale Press, 2010.

▶ Franchino, Vicky. *Sahara Desert*. Ann Arbor, MI: Cherry Lake Publishing, 2016.

Music

▶ Group Bombino. *Guitars from Agadez (Music of Niger)*, *volume 2*. Seattle, WA: Sublime Frequencies, 2009.

▶ Ismaël Lo. *Dabah*. Paris: Disc'Az France, 2006.

▶ Tal National. *Zoy Zoy*. Brighton, England: FatCat Records, 2015.

▶ Visit this Scholastic Web site for more information on Niger:
www.factsfornow.scholastic.com
Enter the keyword **Niger**

Index

Page numbers in *italics*
indicate illustrations.

Zinder and, 27
health care, 37, 89–90, 89, 113, *117*
High Court of Justice, 65
hippopotamuses, *28*, 31
historical maps. *See also* maps.
  Empires, *45*
  European Colonization, *47*
  Shrinking Lake Chad, *25*
holidays
  national, 115
  religious, 94, 98–100
horses, *44, 45*, 88
housing, 27, *27*, 76, 82, 83, 117–119, *117*, 123

I

imams (Muslim leader), 96
imports, 77
imzad (musical instrument), *106*
independence, 13, 49
In-Gall, 113
insect life, 31, *31*, 32, 34
irrigation, 23, 25
Islamic religion. *See also* religion.
  Boko Haram extremist group, 53, *53*
  customary courts and, 66
  death customs, 126–127
  Eid al-Adha holiday, 99–100
  Eid al-Fitr holiday, 97, 99
  five pillars, 96–98
  folk art and, 107
  government and, 66
  Grand Mosque, 97
  hajj (pilgrimage), 98, *98*
  holidays, 94, 98–100
  imams (Muslim leader), 96
  Korité holiday, 99
  Lailatul-Qadr holiday, 99
  Mali and, 44
  mosques, 27, 67, 93, *93*, 97
  Mouloud holiday, 100

Muhammad (Muslim prophet), 96, 100
Muharram (holy month), 99
prayer, 95, 96, 97, *97*, 127
Qur'an, 11, 93, *93*, 96
Ramadan (holy month), *94*, 96, *96*, 97
women and, 95, 101
Zarma-Songhai people and, 82
Islamic University of Niger, 125
Issoufou, Mahamadou, 53, 58, *58*, 61
Ivory Coast, 92

J

Jacquet, Robert, 63
jerboas, 35
jewelry, 41, 87, 107–108
judicial branch of government, 62, 64–65

K

kakaki (musical instrument), 105, *105*
Kanouri language, 93
Kanuri-Manga people, 81, 82, *82*, 88–89
Kiffian people, *40*, 41
Komadougou Yobé River, 23
kora (musical instrument), 105–106
Korité holiday, 99
Kountché, Seyni, 50, 51
kukkuma (musical instrument), 105

L

Lailatul-Qadr holiday, 99
Lake Chad, 25, *25*
land area, 15, 17
languages, 10–11, 12, 13, *13*, 47, 50, 57, 81, 85, 90–93, *91*, 124
"La Nigérienne" (national anthem), 63
La Voix du Sahel radio station, 93
laws, 58, 61, 122

legislative branch of government, 51, *54*, 55, 58, 59–61, *60*, 62, 64, 65, 66
leisure time, 119, *119*, 120–121
Lele, Dan, *109*
L'Exilé (film), 111
Libya, 16
life expectancy, 89
limestone, 75
literacy rate, 92
livestock, *10*, 19, 20, 41, 59, 71, 73, *73*, 86, 88, 113, 125, 126
local governments, 65–66, 66
locusts, 31, *31*
Lô, Ismaël, 107

M

magistrates, 62, 64–65
mail service, *48*
Mali, 16, 44, *45*, 70
mangoes, 126, *126*
Mangou, Sarraounia, 47, 133
manufacturing, 75, 76–77
maps. *See also* historical maps.
  ethnic groups, *82*
  Niamey, *67*
  political, *11*
  population density, *81*
  resources, *71*
  topographical, *17*
marabout (spiritual leader), 79, *79*, 122
Maradi, 27, 80, *127*
marriage, 81, 82, 84, *111*, 113, 116, 121–123, *127*
massifs, 21, *21*
Merkel, Angela, *57*
military, *44, 45*, 50, 58, 59
military coups, 50, 51, *52*, 53
Military Territory of Zinder, 47
millet, *19*, 68, 69, 72, 125
mining, 74–75, *74*

missionaries, 101
Moctar, Mdou, 107, 111
mosques, 27, 67, 93, *93, 97*
motorcycles, 85
Mouloud holiday, 100
Mount Idoûkâl-n-Taghès, 16, 17
mourning, 127
Moussa, Zara, 107
movies, 47, 110–111, 121, 133
Muhammad (Muslim prophet), 96, 100
Muharram (Muslim holy month), 99
music, 63, *102, 104,* 105–107, *105, 106*

N

naming ceremonies, 87, 122
national anthem, 63
National Assembly, 51, *54,* 55, 58, 60, *62,* 65
national flag, 56, *56,* 63
national holidays, 115
National Movement for a Developing Society (MNSD) Party, 51, 55
National Museum of Niger, 37, 67
national parks, 17, 37–38
nature reserves, 37–38, *38*
Niamey. *See also* cities.
    Abdou Moumouni University, 124–125
    average salary in, 71
    Christianity in, *101*
    climate in, 17, 25–26
    education in, *123*
    elections in, 56
    establishment of, 67
    French colonization and, 67
    map of, *67*
    marketplaces in, *124*
    military in, *52, 59*
    National Museum of Niger, 37
    Niger River, *23*

population of, 27, 67, *67,* 80, *80*
    theater, 110
Nigeria, 9, 16, 23, 25, 27, 77, 92
Nigerien Democratic Movement for an African Federation, 55
Nigerien Party for Democracy and Socialism, 55, 60, *61*
Niger River, 16, 17, 23, *23,* 28, 31, 46, 56
notaires, 65, *65*

O

oases, 9, 16, *22*
Office of Radio and Television of Niger, 93
Olympic Games, 110, *110,* 133
ostriches, 38
Ottoman Empire, 45
Oumarou, Mamane, 50
Ousmane, Mahamane, 52

P

Park, Mungo, 46
Parti Progressiste Nigérien (PPN), 49
people. *See also* Fulani people; Hausa people; Tuareg people; women; Zarma-Songhai people.
    Azna, 47
    births, 122
    Bornu, *44,* 45, *45,* 133
    caste system, 86, 115–116
    children, 69, 80, *80,* 87, *87, 93,* 117, 122, *123*
    clothing, 48, 50, 78, 83–84, 95
    corvée system, *48*
    dance, 99, *100,* 110, *111*
    education, 9, 10–13, 47, 50, 69, *91, 93,* 123–125, *123*
    employment, 71
    families, 88–89, 117, 122, 123, 127

food, *12,* 13, 19, 37, 39, 68, 69, 70–71, 76, 77, 90, 95, 97, *124,* 125–126, *126,* 127
    games, *120,* 121
    health care, 37, 89–90, *89,* 113, *117*
    household budget, 76
    housing, 27, *27,* 76, 82, 83, 117–119, *117,* 123
    Kanuri-Manga, 82, 88–89
    Kiffians, *40,* 41
    languages, 10–11, 12, 13, *13,* 47, 50, 57, 81, 85, 90–93, *91,* 124
    leisure time, 119, *119,* 120–121
    life expectancy, 89
    literacy rate, 92
    marriage, 81, 82, 84, *111,* 113, 116, 121–123, *127*
    mourning, 127
    naming ceremonies, 87, 122
    population, 27, 67, 80, *81*
    poverty, 70–71, 90
    slavery, 76
    Songhai Empire, 44, 45, *45*
    tattoos, 86, 87
    Tenerians, 41
    voting rights, *56,* 57, 116
    Wodaabe, 86, *108,* 114, *114*
petroglyphs, 18, *18*
Peul people. *See* Fulani people.
plant life
    Aïr Mountains, 34
    animal life and, 20
    conservation, 36–37, 37–39, *39*
    desertification and, 20
    gueltas, 22, 34–35
    oases, *22*
    reforestation program, 36–37, *39,* 69, 73
    Sahara Desert, 30, 34
    Sahel region, 25, 30
    trees, 33, *33,* 37, *37,* 69

veiling, *78, 79*, 95
women, 12, *12*, 83–85, *84, 104,*
106

U
University of Niamey, 67
uranium mining, 74, *74*, 77

V
villages. *See also* cities; towns.
architecture in, *118*
caste system in, 115
Dallol Bosso and, 24–25
social classes in, 115
Tahoua, *118*
virga rain, 18
voting rights, *56*, 57, 116
Voulet, Paul, *46*, 47

W
wadis (riverbeds), 18, 24
water, 24–25, *24*, 34–35, *116*, 118
waterfall, 22
wells, 24–25, *24*
West African franc (currency), 70, *70*
wildlife. *See* animal life; insect life;
plant life; reptilian life.
W National Park, 39
Wodaabe people, 86, *108*, 114, *114*
women. *See also* people.
death customs and, 127
education and, 125
government and, *54, 60*

Islamic religion and, 95, 101 , 127
marriage, 125, *127*
music and, *104*
Sarraounia Mangou, 47, 133
status, of, 116
Tuareg, 12, *12*, 83–85, *84, 104, 106*
water and, *116*, 118
work of, 116–117, *116*, 118
wrestling, 109, *109*

X
xalam (musical instrument), 106

Z
Zarma-Songhai people. See also
people
agriculture, 82
animism and, 101
language, 90, 91, 93, 124
map, *82*
marriage, 82
percentage of, 81
population of, 82
storytelling, 103–104
zebus, 30, *30*, 73
Zinder. *See also* cities.
architecture, 27, *27*
education in, *93*, 125
French colonization of, 47
marketplace, 27
mosques in, *93*
population of, 27, 80

Meet the Author

BARBARA SOMERVILL HAS BEEN writing children's nonfiction books for more than twenty years. She writes about countries, earth science, biographies, and social studies. Somervill teaches college writing and critical reading classes. When not teaching or writing, she loves movies, theater, baking, and softball.

Photo Credits